Three voices of art therapy: ima therapist

The 'three voices' of art therapy – the image, the client and the therapist – are essential aspects of the art therapy relationship. In this powerful story the client, Kim Terry, describes his own path from depression to health and creativity through a series of extraordinary images.

When art therapist Gabrielle Rifkind first met Kim, he was withdrawn, isolated, had suicidal thoughts, and was encased in a metaphorical 'suit of armour' to protect himself. In weekly art therapy sessions over two years, he began slowly to work through his difficulties, to face the real world, and, by exploring his own creativity, to learn to live with himself.

This account provides an exceptional opportunity to hear the voice of the client as well as that of the therapist. It becomes clear how deep a relationship Gabrielle and Kim enter over the course of the therapeutic encounter. Therapy and process 'come alive' in the descriptive text, which addresses the reality of the two individuals' experience and their reciprocal difficulties.

The most permanent and powerful voice in the text, as in art therapy, is that of the images which are chosen to represent the stages of Kim's therapeutic experience. They richly express the issues with which he was struggling at the time and clearly illustrate his process of change. They are deliberately repeated in the book to convey the centrality of the image in the art therapy process and its emphasis on visual rather than verbal communication.

An additional voice, outside the therapeutic relationship, is provided by Tessa Dalley. She gives an objective, theoretical view of the process as it occurs and, by drawing together the inter-relationship between the three voices, adds to the understanding of what is happening in the session.

Three Voices of Art Therapy is written for professionals, but it is also intended to span a wider readership and reach out to those who might find themselves in a similar situation to Kim or who are thinking of embarking on an art therapy experience for themselves. Such a fully rounded account of clinical practice in art therapy is rarely available. The common dilemmas and issues which it describes will be of interest to professional and non-professional reader alike.

Tessa Dalley is a senior art therapist working at Parkside Clinic, London; **Gabrielle Rifkind** is an art therapist and group analyst working in the NHS and in private practice; **Kim Terry** is a senior graphic designer with a West London design consultancy.

Three voices of art therapy: image, client, therapist

Tessa Dalley, Gabrielle Rifkind and Kim Terry

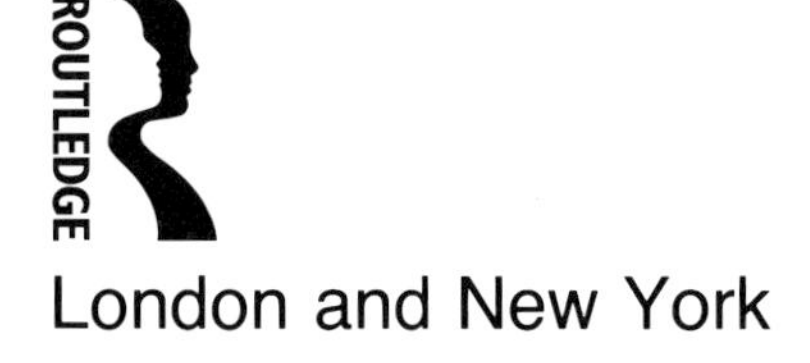

London and New York

First published 1993
by Routledge
11 New Fetter Lane, London EC4P 4EE

Simultaneously published in the USA and Canada
by Routledge
29 West 35th Street, New York, NY 10001

Typeset in Times by J&L Composition Ltd, Filey, North Yorkshire
Printed and bound in Great Britain by
Biddles Ltd, Guildford and King's Lynn

British Library Cataloguing in Publication Data
A catalogue record for this book is available from the British Library.

Library of Congress Cataloging in Publication Data
Dalley, Tessa.
Three voices of art therapy: image, client, therapist/Tessa Dalley, Gabrielle Rifkind, and Kim Terry.
p. cm.
Includes bibliographical references and index.
1. Art therapy – Case studies. 2. Terry, Kim – Mental health.
3. Depressed persons – Rehabilitation – Case studies. I. Rifkind, Gabrielle, 1953– . II. Terry, Kim. III. Title.
RC489.A7D25 1993
616.8′5156 – dc20 93–16768
CIP

ISBN 0-415-07795-8 (hbk)
ISBN 0-415-07796-6 (pbk)

Style Junkie

'You can imagine what it might be like to live with someone you don't like. Basically you wouldn't do it, you would ask them to leave or even move out yourself. But what if you can do neither, what if the person you despise and hate is yourself.'

Kim Terry, 1988

Contents

Illustrations

All figures are also reproduced as colour plates.

The authors

Tessa Dalley is an experienced art therapist working part-time in the Child and Parent Department of Parkside Clinic. She also works as a supervisor for other practising art therapists and in private practice. Tessa is on the teaching staff on the Postgraduate Diploma Course in Art Therapy, Goldsmiths' College, and has published several books.

Gabrielle Rifkind is an art therapist and group analyst. She works in the NHS and in private practice and runs several groups in the community. She also works professionally as an artist and is particularly interested in how images and words can facilitate emotional literacy.

Kim Terry is a practising graphic designer. Since he qualified, he has had a wide range of experience working for commercial companies and on a freelance basis. At the moment he is working and living in West London.

Foreword

Kim Terry

My association with this project arose out of my treatment at Parkside Clinic. Severe depression lost me my career and relationships, leaving me with no reason in my life for carrying on in the face of the struggle each day had become. Therapy had been of little help in the past, but when it was suggested that I could attend art therapy I thought I had nothing to lose. I believed this to be my last chance.

The sessions helped me to regain my confidence in being able to control my life as well as making me realise I am a creative individual. This has been a cornerstone in the development of myself from a point where I thought I had none. I gained my qualification in graphic design while still attending therapy. This makes me optimistic that the rest of my life will not take me to the dead end I arrived at before.

I now take pleasure in drawing and painting because I have learnt to express myself. Prior to art therapy my pictures were cold and emotionless and could have been done by a computer.

My main motivation for this project is to share my own personal experience with people with a similar struggle, as well as therapists. I would not be where I am today without it.

Chapter 1

Introduction

This book emerged out of a two-year relationship with a patient in art therapy who produced a series of extraordinary images. It is an important and powerful story to tell because it is a young man's path from depression to health and creativity.

When the art therapist Gabrielle Rifkind first met Kim, he was withdrawn, isolated and suicidal, encased in a metaphorical 'suit of armour' to protect himself. He presented himself as someone in crisis, feeling trapped in his loneliness, confused and full of self-loathing. Through the process of weekly art therapy sessions, he slowly began to work through his difficulties, to face the real world and, by exploring his own creativity, to learn to live with himself.

What was exceptional about Kim's experience in art therapy was both the strength of communication in his images and his ability to describe them. Within five months, Kim started to keep a diary of what was happening for him and so he found both a visual and a verbal communication to describe his experience. It was a powerful example of releasing the painful internal world and gaining some mastery of it. As he began to demonstrate his capacity to communicate his thoughts, feelings and fantasies in images and in written words, this provided the means through which he could articulate them within the therapeutic relationship. He had found a 'language'. This enabled him to move from a position of emotional 'autism' to emotional 'literacy'. By this we mean that Kim had neither the emotional vocabulary nor the insight to be able to describe his experience of confusion, powerlessness and little sense of self. The therapeutic process increased the self-awareness of his psychological world and he found a language to describe it, leading to his emotional literacy (Orbach 1989). This combination of factors was to set the foundations of a book which we wanted to write together four years after Kim first came to therapy.

Kim was keen to put his experience in writing so that he might be able to help or communicate with others in the same state of desperation as himself. Kim has chosen not to reveal his own name. He wanted to remain anonymous for the sake of future job prospects and out of respect to his family. This decision was carefully reached among ourselves. The dilemma for us was that, in the process of the therapy, Kim had worked so intensively to uncover false masks in his attempt to find his real self. We wondered whether the act of taking a pseudonym would increase his vulnerability to this old process and reinforce the idea of a false persona. However, Kim felt that he had moved beyond this. Moreover, we felt the experience of Mary Barnes, where she used her real name, has left her a client forever.

FORMAT OF *THREE VOICES*

The book is entitled *Three Voices* as three essential aspects of an art therapy relationship will be taken into account. The triangle of voices speaks to us from the client, Kim, the art therapist, Gabrielle, and the image. Generally, in the analysis of the process of therapeutic relationships, so often we hear the voice of the therapist or occasionally that of the client. 'Reports given by patients are of particular importance. Psychotherapists need to learn from their clients and it is regrettable that, despite a plethora of descriptions of the psychotherapeutic process from therapists, there are relatively few from patients' (Meares and Hobson 1977: 50). In this study we will be making links between all three components of the art therapy relationship. Connecting the three voices will enable us to explore where the patient and therapist share the same experience, and how at particular times they saw and felt things differently. We also have the most permanent and powerful voice, that of the image which will speak to all of us in different ways.

Each chapter begins with an image. The thirteen pictures are chosen out of over fifty that Kim produced over the period of two years and represent the stages of his therapeutic experience. The colour plates will be found towards the back of the book, but connections between the image and the writing will constantly be made as both are powerful communications. The images are rich examples of the issues with which Kim was struggling at the time and clearly illustrate his process of change. There is no inclusion of detailed process notes but the material has been put together under one theme which is illustrated by the image. Where necessary, we have made reference to other pictures he produced but the emphasis on the images serves to convey how the visual communication, and the centrality of the image in the process, is the powerful catalyst for change and is essential to the message we wish to communicate.

In addition to the three voices within the therapeutic relationship, an outer voice, that of Tessa Dalley, will provide an additional, objective view by drawing together the interrelationship between these three voices with some theoretical consideration of the process as it occurs. This sets up another triad – the patient, the therapist and the outside observer. The last of these will pay attention to the outer and inner voices of both patient and therapist through the images and words, and, in this way, the process of each session will be explored in depth. Her role enables an analysis of the developing process between patient, therapist and image which will resonate, as a type of supervisory relationship, by adding to the clarification and understanding of the material. The overview is not meant to be understood as the 'definitive statement'; rather to offer a different aspect to the thinking about process and hopefully offer some clarity. An objective view of process leads to a fuller understanding which in turn can raise further questions and issues to think about. There are many different ways of looking at clinical material and any therapist in supervision will be familiar with this process.

This structure is both simple and complex. The descriptions of the experience of sessions as they occurred between therapist and client have been written entirely independently and then come together in the text. As three years have elapsed since the treatment ended, the material is derived from memory, diary entries, recollection of events over time and process notes. The analysis of this by the outer voice provides the theoretical framework for an understanding of the process after the termination of treatment. This has enabled an interesting insight into the different perceptions and understandings that develop during the writing and this again is the focus for comment. The final chapter will provide an up-to-date account of the experience by way of the transcript of a recorded three-way dialogue between Gabrielle, Kim and Tessa, three live voices coming together in their recollection of the process of the treatment and how it looked in hindsight.

We hope this will provide an insight into the art therapeutic process which is rarely available in such detail. This case is unusual in that the client was interested in becoming a designer and so we have not only the process of the sessions but some skilfully executed images to illustrate this. Most clients in art therapy are not so accomplished in their technical skill, and indeed most of them have not used art materials since their experience of art lessons at school. This is not, of course, a measure of whether the client can work therapeutically, but Kim's obvious artistic talent adds a particular dimension to the work. What we are hoping to address is the central question for art therapists of how the combination of the image, the therapist and the client and their mutual understanding facilitates growth and change. This account is basically descriptive, as the theory and ideas of process are easier to understand if the therapist and client 'come alive' in the text and address the reality of their individual experience and the reciprocal difficulties that each sets up in the other. For this reason, it makes sense for us to place this story in a social context. We recognise that Kim's experience is located in a culture that includes his immediate and extended family, his educational culture, peer group and the value system that surrounded being white and growing up in Britain in the 1960s. So when we examine processes within the text we will be holding all this in mind in terms of their social context. For example, the examination of the mother–son relationship is within the context of a Western culture and patterns of parenting where the mother is, initially, the centre of gravity.

Over the course of the therapeutic encounter, Gabrielle and Kim enter a depth of relationship that this case illustrates. Working within a therapeutic relationship is essentially a private experience. It is difficult to translate it into a public arena as one is usually unprepared to do so. We hope the experience has not been lost in the act of translation. In writing this, there is a sense of our practice being put up for scrutiny and oneself being laid open for comment. However, we feel that we can contribute to the on-going development of our professional understanding through a project of this nature and were therefore keen to undertake it. Anyone working in the caring professions can understand this dilemma of how much clinical practice to share together and how much to hold back. We would argue for open and honest debate and constructive and creative dialogue in the sharing of what we perceive to be current issues and dilemmas common to most practitioners. In this sense, it is up to the reader to formulate their own view of the case.

As will become clear, different models are used for understanding, and this dialogue and exchange of ideas has been important in re-examining our thinking about this work. We have felt this was a creative way to proceed and has helped us understand that there is no 'right' way to do things. Every aspect of the therapeutic process is taken into consideration as all therapists struggle with the complexities of the communications, conflicts and preoccupations that the client is trying to convey.

It is also clear that without clarity of purpose there is always the possibility of misunderstanding. Theoretical positions can be set up in isolation where there are not always the same internal and external frames of reference. Dialogue provided sufficient space for all our ideas and the anchorage has been to listen and understand each other's communication. In any discussion, anxiety can fill up the space for thinking, giving no room for the other person's ideas. We found it was possible to make sense of the other's understanding and at the same time to differentiate ourselves and hold on to our own particular meaning. In a sense, this task mirrored Kim's task in therapy and parallels the 'therapeutic experience'. Real growth comes when the person in therapy is able to have a sufficiently clear sense of self that they are able to differentiate themselves in relationship to the other. This is not the same as seeing onself as different in a way which has not involved the understanding of the experience.

We hope this book will have a wide readership. While it will be of great interest to art therapists and students, we hope it will resonate with our professional colleagues with whom we work closely, such as social workers, psychiatrists, psychologists, psychotherapists. It is also our intention to span a wider readership and reach out to those interested in the subject as a means both of identification and of stimulation. It may be for some people a catalyst for their own self-expression. For others there may be recognition of themselves which might lead to a connection with an art therapeutic experience.

One of the most interesting aspects of working on a project of this type was the degree to which the voices informed and were informed by each other in the process of the writing. This theme will be further developed in the next chapter in terms of the theoretical perspectives that were there at the start and also how we became aware of some differences in clinical practice and approach which have been central to the dialogue throughout. Any notion of difference has thus been worked with and integrated. We therefore feel that this style of writing opens a creative debate to many different disciplines, but also addresses differences within practising professionals of the same discipline.

Chapter 2

The context of practice

Some theoretical considerations

First, we would like to put this clinical material into the theoretical context in which our practice is based. Art therapy is the use of art materials within the context of a psychotherapeutic relationship. The images produced provide the focus through which a patient can express and work through the issues and concerns that have brought him or her into therapy. The art therapist and client work together to understand the art process and product of the session and this forms the basis for a triangular relationship. Many clients find it easier to relate to the therapist through the art object which, as a personal statement, provides a focus for discussion, analysis and self-evaluation. It is concrete and therefore acts as a record of the therapeutic process that cannot be denied, erased or forgotten and offers possibilities for reflection and further understanding in the future. The transference that develops within the relationship between therapist and client is also incorporated into the art work, giving a valuable 'third dimension' or three-way communication.

Within the current art therapy literature, different perspectives in theory and practice with various client groups are discussed and explored in depth (Dalley 1984; Dalley *et al.* 1987; Case and Dalley 1990, 1992; Schaverien 1992; Simon 1992). For the purposes of this chapter, an introduction to aspects of art therapy theory that are in evidence in the text will be considered. In particular, Schaverien's work on analytical art psychotherapy has developed an understanding of the transference processes involved in image making and their importance within the therapy session which is of particular interest throughout this case.

As will become clear, art therapy involves using images to facilitate the unfolding and understanding of psychic processes by providing a setting in which connections with previously repressed, unconscious material can surface. Associations and feelings from the past can emerge through the imagery while the art therapist, as artist and psychotherapist, allows an understanding of this process. The ability of the art therapist to provide this setting depends on her capacity to understand its importance which stems from her personal knowledge of how it feels to create images in the same way as her patients. Her own experience in personal therapy will assist her in the understanding and consideration of boundaries and transference relationships.

Art therapists vary in the emphasis they place on the importance of the inner dialogue of the patient's own creative activity and how this process is then understood in the analysis of the art product itself within the outer dialogue between therapist and client. It is generally agreed that both aspects of the art therapeutic process are equally important but it is the focus on the image which essentially separates us from our psychotherapy colleagues.

The therapeutic contract entered into between art therapist and client involves the time of the session, where it will take place and how long over time this arrangement will continue. These boundaries establish the frame inside which therapeutic work occurs. The session becomes a safe space in which feelings and thoughts are allowed to emerge. Within this outer frame, the picture is created and this setting is the frame which contains, holds and exhibits the picture and the patient's relation to it.

> Within the outer frame there is an inner space in which many things happen, including the making of pictures. It is within this frame that the transference to the therapist and to the picture may emerge. It is within this frame that a reciprocal countertransference may develop. This is the inner sanctum of the analytical art psychotherapy setting. The 'picture within the frame' is the picture which is created within the framed space of the room and the relationship. This is like a vessel, which offers an additional type of framed space, this time particular to the patient. This is space apart from the therapist; it is private space in which the patient can explore, play, experiment and form relationships, in ways in which are personal to her or him. It offers a way of relating to the self, or parts of the self, and even at times an opportunity for self-analysis within the bounds of the paper.
>
> (Schaverien 1992: 65)

We therefore have a 'picture' of the therapeutic space. If the art therapist maintains the safe space for the client, then the therapeutic process will become established. As the outer boundaries remain constant, Schaverien describes how the picture, which is safely contained within the boundaries of the edge of the paper, reveals the imaginal world. This may contain unmanageable, chaotic, unacceptable, as well as previously unexpressed, feelings and images. The picture may be constantly changing which allows the therapist and client to become aesthetically and emotionally connected to the picture and work through its significance. The task of the art therapist is to be receptive and tolerant to all aspects of the client's experience. These must be understood in terms of the present – the here and now of the situation – but also in terms of the client's past, particularly in terms of the client's early experience as an infant. As the focus of the session is narrowed onto the image and onto the person of the therapist, early infantile experiences of original relationships will be explored in the transference relationship.

Transference occurs when the patient transfers strong, infantile feelings that originate from childhood experiences or early relations onto the therapist. For art therapists, there is a need to understand how the transference relationship is affected by the introduction of the art object. The image often becomes the focus through which the transference relationship is explored. It holds the significance of feeling in that it acts as a receptacle for the phantasies, anxieties and other unconscious processes that are now emerging into consciousness for the client in therapy. It therefore contains aspects of the transference but a separate response also takes place in terms of the painting in its own right.

> These pictures produce an empowered form of relating which draws the artist/patient and therapist/viewer into a deep transference to the picture itself; and also to each other through the picture. In these pictures, that which usually remains unseen, unstated, even unconscious, between people is evident and cannot be completely denied. The purpose of therapy is to mediate in the divided, inner world of the patient and the picture offers a means of just such mediation.
>
> (Schaverien 1992: 23)

We are thus concerned with the presence of an image within the therapy relationship for both client and therapist. Both transference and counter-transference develop through the response to the image itself. Counter-transference is the therapist's own feeling response to the client and the image in a therapy situation. The therapist's feeling responses can be understood as a useful indicator of the client's experience and feelings, and there is thus a need for the therapist to differentiate these from her own personal agenda. Bion (1962) formulated a clear understanding of the therapist as a container for the client's intolerable experiences. He developed the idea of the therapist as a maternal container – by being able to discern something of what is wrong, the important ego function involved in mothering, the therapist can respond in such a way as to relieve some of the distress.

This 'model' of maternal containment gives a clear account of how the counter-transference is an important instrument for understanding the therapeutic process and is certainly useful for our own understanding of this clinical material. Both therapist and patient will feel a whole range of feelings and responses to the images produced and this indicates the multiplicity of feelings that are being conveyed. Feelings, phantasies, thoughts which occur to the therapist in the therapeutic relationship and through the image are evoked as a response to the client's transference.

If this is accepted and acknowledged, it deepens the client's relation to the unconscious which is also held in the imagery.

It is within this transference and counter-transference response to the image that the complexity of the art therapy process lies. 'The process is one of "mirroring" reverberating and reflecting back and forth through several layers of consciousness; the consciousness of the object, of the artist, who creates the presentation of the self through the object or in the object and of the beholder, who responds to all the layers with accumulation of conscious and unconscious associations which include deeply private nodal points in the unique experience in which there are correspondences, but not identities in others' (Kuhns 1983: 21).

Schaverien's idea of 'diagrammatical' and 'embodied' images, and the subsequent feeling states that these contain, develops this understanding of the centrality of the image and the transference relation to it. She discusses the idea of the 'scapegoat' transference in the client's relation to the image, as scapegoating is a form of splitting. By separating the 'good' from the 'bad' and the subsequent disposal of the 'bad' the ritual is completed and the opportunity of resolution comes into effect once the scapegoat has been disposed of. Connected to this, the idea of the talisman as a magically empowered object is central to Schaverien's thinking. The embodied image becomes magically empowered, like a talisman, as the image becomes invested with the transference process. These important concepts will be further elaborated when they can be seen to be occurring within the process; they are clearly illustrated in this material.

The importance of interpretation in art therapy needs some consideration here. The complexity of the making unconscious processes conscious through interpretation has been discussed at length by Bion, Winnicott and later analysts and their ideas have helped us, as art therapists, a great deal in our thinking. Like the mother, the therapist facilitates by providing opportunity for communication and its recognition. By waiting, free from judgement, the therapist remains open to the client's own interpretations. This is particularly important in the presence of images, the meaning of which might on the surface seem obvious, but the art therapist must wait to hear from the painting client as to the significance and meaning for them of the image. Winnicott (1963) makes the connection between interpretation and feeding, as the mother interprets the infant's cry for hunger, so the therapist's verbal interpretation can be like a feed in language for the client. However, he warns against the dangers of premature interpretation which can be an experience that does not allow the client to hear or 'take in' and in this sense language is potentially a terrifying maternal object (Winnicott 1963). Winnicott implies that language, in the form of an accurate interpretation for which the client is not ready, can reach his innermost being, penetrate the most primitive defences and acquire an unexpected potency:

> Here there is danger if the analyst interprets instead of waiting for the patient to creatively discover. If we wait we become objectively perceived in the patients' own time, but if we fail to behave in a way that is facilitating the patient's analytic process (which is equivalent to the infant and child's maturational process) we suddenly become not-me for the patient and then we know too much, and we are dangerous because we are too nearly in communication with the central still and silent spot of the patients' ego-organisation.
>
> (Winnicott 1963: 189)

Sensitive and timely interpretation would seem to be crucial in the process of art therapy. One aspect of the work of interpretation is to lead to the reconstruction of the client's past but, during this, there may be an increase in the level of distress and pain as previously hidden feelings and buried aspects of self become uncovered. One of the tasks of being in therapy is to be able to withstand this and work it through.

Working through is an important process that is central to our practice and involves attending therapy even when it is difficult. It means enabling the client to experience his feelings, anxieties and past situations over and over again in relation both to the therapist and to different people and situations in his past and present life. However painful, uncomfortable or confusing an experience, if the client can stay with these difficult feelings, some understanding will take place and a more resolved position will be reached. Normal patterns of behaviour, such as running away and avoiding conflict, may be used in an attempt to block out the emotional pain, but this merely compounds the problems with the repetition of previous patterns of relating. As Sandler *et al.* (1973) point out, working through is additional to uncovering conflicts and resistances. Intellectual insight without working through is not regarded as sufficient, as the tendency to repeat previous ways of functioning would remain. Change comes about when the transference relationship has become recognized, which gives the possibility of breaking the pattern of relating.

THREE VOICES

Much of this will be illuminated clearly in the following detailed account of the art therapy relationship. As mentioned earlier, the format of writing with 'Three Voices' allows us to examine closely the evolution of the treatment over time and to explain in detail both practice and theory in this process. For this reason there will not be a complete coverage of the literature, but relevant references will be given in the text. By briefly outlining here fundamental aspects of other psychoanalytic thinking that has helped us, particularly with this clinical material, we hope to establish a wider framework into which the reader can place the work.

DONALD WINNICOTT

Winnicott's contribution to our thinking cannot be overestimated. It is hard to select particular aspects of his work but, with this case in mind, the importance of creativity, the transitional space and the location of cultural experience for the development of the capacity to play and his clarification of early relationships between mother and child have been used extensively throughout the text. His description of an intermediate area of 'experiencing' between inner and outer realities seems central to our understanding. The environment that the mother creates for her infant and her capacity to adapt to stages of independence and separation allow objects to become separate and real. Thus, the infant is helped to develop a capacity to experience a relationship to external reality. It is through this 'intermediate area' of experience that the infant can develop a capacity to be separate from mother through the use of 'transitional objects' and 'transitional phenomena'. The significance of transitional objects for early stages of object relating and early symbol formation is that they allow the infant to feel able to exist within the 'potential space' – neither inside nor outside a person but in the 'place' between them. The 'potential space' becomes the designated safe play area between mother and child which becomes in turn the 'location of cultural experience'.

> This gives us our indication for therapeutic procedure – to afford opportunity for formless experience, and for creative impulses, motor and sensory, which are the stuff of playing. And on the basis of playing is built the whole of man's experiential existence. No longer are we either introvert or extrovert. We experience life in the area of transitional phenomena, in the exciting interweave of subjectivity and objective observation, and in an area that is intermediate between the inner reality of the individual and the shared reality of the world that is external to individuals.
>
> (Winnicott 1981: 75)

Also, Winnicott's formulation of the concepts of true and false self has been equally useful in our understanding of Kim and his experience and it is worth looking at this in detail. The true self is that part of the self that is central and powered by instincts and the false self is that which is turned outwards and is related to the world. Winnicott (1960) describes how this division takes place as the infant's ego is building up strength and getting towards a state in which id demands will be felt as part of the self and not as environmental. 'When this development occurs, the id-satisifaction strengthens the True Self. But id excitements can be traumatic when the ego is not yet able to include them, and not yet able to contain the risks involved and the frustrations experienced up to the point when id-satisfaction becomes a fact' (Winnicott 1960: 141).

Normally the true self is protected but has some life and the false self is the social attitude. The false self functions as a defence to hide and protect the true self. The false self sets itself up as real and people think that this is the real person. When the false self becomes exploited and treated as real there is a growing sense in the individual of futility and despair. 'At the extreme of abnormality, the false self can easily get itself mistaken for real so that the real self is under threat of annihilation. Suicide can then be a reassertion of the true self' (Winnicott 1960: 133).

Winnicott introduced the idea of the 'good enough' mother to explain the aetiology of the false self and it becomes clear how Kim struggled with this in his early experience.

> The good enough mother meets the omnipotence of the infant and to some extent makes sense of it. She does this repeatedly. A True self begins to have life, through the strength given to the infant's weak ego by the mother's implementation of the infant's omnipotent expressions.
>
> The mother who is not good enough is not able to implement the infant's omnipotence, and so she repeatedly fails to meet the infant gesture, instead she substitutes her own gesture which is to be given sense by the compliance of the infant. This compliance on the part of the infant is the earliest state of the False self and belongs to the mother's inability to sense her infant's needs.
>
> (Winnicott 1960: 145)

In the extreme examples of false self development, the true self is so well hidden that spontaneity is not a feature in the infant's living experience. Compliance is the main feature, with imitation as a speciality. It is possible to trace the point of origin of the false self, which can now be seen to be a defence against that which is unthinkable, the exploitation of the true self which would result in annihilation. Winnicott describes the clinical application of this concept where the therapist can only talk to the false self of the client about the client's true self. At the point of transition when the therapist begins to get into contact with the client's true self, there must be a period of extreme dependence. He comments that more headway is made by recognition of the client's non-existence than by a long continued working with the client on the basis of ego defence mechanisms. 'The false self lacks something and that something is the essential central element of creative originality' (Winnicott 1960: 152). The true self is the personal idea or spontaneous gesture; only the true self can be creative and feel real.

WILFRED BION

Bion formulated ideas of containment and the importance of the therapist as a container for the client's intolerable experiences. This containment, and the mother's role of giving meaning to experiences, allows the acquisition, inside the infant, of an internal object that has the capacity to understand these experiences. By putting these experiences into words, meaning is generated.

Bion's constructs to do with thinking help us to understand the client's experience (Bion 1961). From birth the baby has inborn preconceptions such as the breast but no preconceptions of a breast that satisfies. Once he has an actual experience of a satisfying breast, this links the feeling of the satisfaction with the preconception. As this is positive, there is emotional affect and the experience is kept and stored for future reference. This creates the concept of learning from experience. However, if the meeting of a preconception and the real event is not a positive experience, then Bion suggests the emotional experience becomes unbearable and is evacuated (Bion 1977).

The capacity to learn from experience is essential in healthy ego development and Bion introduces the notion of alpha and beta functioning. This can be understood from the following example:

> To learn from experience alpha function must operate on the awareness of the emotional experience, alpha elements are produced from the impressions of the experience; these are thus made storable and available for dream thoughts and for unconscious waking thinking. A child having the emotional experience called learning to walk is able by virtue of alpha function to store this experience. Thought that had originally to be conscious becomes unconscious and so the child can do all the thinking needed for walking without any longer being conscious of any of it. Alpha function is needed for conscious thinking and reasoning and for the relegation of thinking to the unconscious when it is necessary to disencumber consciousness of the burden of thought by learning a skill. If there are only beta elements, which cannot be made unconscious, there can be no repressions, suppressions or learning.
>
> (Bion 1962: 13)

MELANIE KLEIN, HANNA SEGAL, MARION MILNER

These ideas provide a framework for understanding both Kim's experience and also the shifts he makes during the therapy. These can be understood according to different theoretical perspectives. Adults in therapy tend to relive early infantile experiences and the emphasis placed on this largely depends on how this is understood, particularly in terms of ego development. Throughout this study, the overview brings a broadly Kleinian view to the material, understanding how, in ego development, the baby moves between the paranoid–schizoid position and the depressive position.

From birth, the baby deals with destructive impulses by splitting processes. Splitting can be understood to be an internalised form of relating to the outer world. Idealisation and denial enable the feelings of love and hate towards the first object, the breast, to be kept separate. Bad parts are projected onto an object/mother by whom the baby then feels persecuted, but as the depressive position is reached there is a realisation that love and hate are directed towards the same object and mother is experienced as a whole object. This gives rise to sadness and guilt at earlier attacks and a sense of the whole object being damaged by these attacks. The infant experiences desolation, feeling that the hateful feelings have destroyed the good breast, and feels loss and guilt (Klein 1957).

This leads to a desire to restore and recreate the lost loved object and these reparative impulses, Segal (1975) argues, contribute to good relationships, for sublimation to work and are a fundamental drive to all artistic creativity. Segal's work on symbol formation, developed from Klein's work on symbolism, is also of interest as Kim struggles to communicate his experience. Distinguishing symbol formation in the paranoid–schizoid position and in the depressive position, she describes how the symbol is initially confused with the object, but in the depressive position there is greater awareness of differentiation and separateness between ego and object and recognition of ambivalence towards the object; the symbol, a creation of the ego, is recognised as separate from the object (Segal 1957).

Marion Milner, who played a central role in the enquiry into art and psychoanalysis, adds to the discussion. Milner, like Winnicott, saw the need for experience of a non-purposive state, a ticking over of the unintegrated personality, experience of formlessness. She suggests this needs to be reflected back, a role that is performed by mother in infancy and the therapist in treatment. This is the mirror role of mother and therapist and has relevance for both art and play:

> In play, there is something half way between day dreaming and purposeful instinctive or experimental action. As soon as a child has moved a toy in response to some wish or fantasy, then the scene created by play is different and a new situation sets off a new set of possibilities; just as in free imaginative drawings the sight of a mark made on paper provokes new associations, the line, as it were, answers back and functions as a very primitive type of external object.
>
> (Milner 1955: 92)

These ideas will be used extensively to inform the thinking in the writing of the overview. However, what is interesting is that Gabrielle uses a more empathetic approach to her work, focusing less on the internal world and putting the emphasis on a more interactive style in the interface of the outer and inner worlds. This has allowed us to look at both ways of working when considering the process of this therapeutic relationship and there are many points at which there seem to be overlaps where inner and outer worlds meet. For example, this view of mirroring and reflecting back outlined by Milner suggests some similarities with the theories of Kohut on narcissism (1971).

HEINZ KOHUT

The keystone of Kohut's theory of treatment is empathy or vicarious introspection. By this he means the ability to enter into the mind and feelings of the other and then make sense of this in terms of one's own understanding. The basic structure of psychoanalytic self psychology is essentially relational. It is what happens *between* as part of the process and, when it is applied to art therapy, the therapist tries to understand both the experience of the patient and the possible communication of the picture. She reads the picture through the eyes of the client and then enquires. As will become clear, Gabrielle places emphasis on not remaining a 'blank screen' but being available and responsive to the client's communication.

Kohut's self psychology grew out of a clinical experience of patient's suffering from self-depletion and self-fragmentation. He observed that patients experienced a sense of wholeness when they were responded to in an empathetic manner and felt understood. Kohut saw the self object needs as normal developmental needs from birth to death and not as pathological. Healthy, normally functioning people search for self object needs all their lives. Kohut identified narcissistic needs such as the desire for recognition, to be heard, to be taken seriously, to identify with someone, to differentiate ourselves, to idealise and to merge. In Kohut's view, early failure in empathy on the part of parental figures is the primary factor causing narcissistic personality disorders (together with other pre-oedipal problems). 'The equilibrium of primary narcissism is disturbed by the unavoidable shortcomings of maternal care, but the child replaces the previous perfection (a) by establishing a grandiose self and exhibitionistic image of the self, the grandiose self, and (b) by giving over the previous perfection to be admired, omnipotent (transitional) self object: the idealised parent imago' (Kohut 1971: 25). Real others are then objects separate from oneself. Kohut believed that it is through the emphatic response in the therapeutic situation that cure is achieved through cohesion of the self.

Art therapy may be seen to supply the individual with an abundant potential of self object experiences and the possibility of working through many self object needs. It is through the experience of 'empathetic intuneness' both in the relationship and via the image that the client is able to have many of his self object needs met. This seems to have been a central aspect to the relationship between Kim and Gabrielle.

RELATIONAL MATRIX

Lastly, we think it worth considering a different sort of 'baby' from 'Freud's baby' which was seen as a conglomeration of physically based urges. This baby requires certain basic environmental conditions and parental functions for growth and development. The baby/child, and later the adult, is shaped and embedded in a wide matrix with other people. For healthy development it is acknowledged that the baby and then child requires certain conditions which may be seen as being characterised by holding, containing, mirroring, separateness, merger, differentiation and the opportunity for symbolic merger (Mitchell 1988).

The human infant develops through a complex set of social interactions. Relatedness is not a means to an end, to reduce tension or create security. It is the very nature of the infant that draws him into relationships. The individual may be seen to be a rich interaction of his culture, his linguistic environment and his interactions in relationships and from this the infant derives meaning. The child can be seen to learn a mode of connectedness with his family which is maintained throughout his life. The child becomes connected to the parents' character patterns and it is these patterns the child transfers on to his relationships in his adult communications. The basic relational configuration may be seen as three-dimensional – the self, the other and the space between self and other. There is no self outside the matrix of relations with other. This space in art therapy may be seen to be the image and it is the careful exploration of the 'space between' which allows the greater insight into the patient/therapist relationship. It is through this that the person in therapy gains a clear sense of self.

All these ideas and different approaches are useful to hold in mind throughout this study. Most professionals will be familiar with the tensions of working between inner and outer world experience and how there can be room for both in the understanding of the work. The art therapist helps the client to clarify and explore the material they bring. This involves constantly holding the balance between the client's internal world with their fantasies and fears and the real world outside. In this way, therapy can be understood as a means to integrate inner and outer world; it also puts the experience of therapy into context. This provides the notion of building blocks, setting up the inner foundations for change in terms of relationships outside. We can see in the case of Kim how he is able to engage in the intense relationship with the therapist and, as this is worked through, how he was able to translate this to new relationships. The images and his relationship to them are central to this process.

The clinic

The setting for this work was a National Health Service Outclient clinic, which was a consultation and therapy centre for both children and adults. Gabrielle Rifkind worked as the art therapist as a member of the multi-disciplinary team within the adult department of the clinic. This team of psychologists, psychotherapists, social workers, psychiatrists would meet to consider referrals to the clinic and decide what would be the most appropriate response to the needs of the individual concerned. Referrals come from a variety of sources including GPs, social workers and other professionals working in the community. Self-referrals are also quite frequent.

The art therapy room

At the time Kim first came to the clinic, the art therapy room was very small. On the walls there are framed pictures done by clients who have been in therapy. These are put on the wall only with clients' consent and when they are ready to make public their private worlds. The room could be experienced as warm and womblike, or small, swampy and invasive. Clients in the past have commented on it being both. There were two comfy armchairs in the room and a table and a chair in the corner under the window which looked out onto the street. On the table was a range of paints, crayons, pastels, charcoals and pencils. Self-hardening clay was also available. When the client was engaged in image making he would sit at the table with his back to Gabrielle and she would sit in one of the other two chairs. Many art therapists like to sit by the client so they can share the process but as the room was so small this would have felt rather intrusive.

In the next chapter, Kim outlines his view of his developmental history and the therapist's response on their first meeting is given, which sets the two voices of therapist and client in context.

Chapter 3

Developmental history, assessment interview and therapist's first impressions

'A child of the seventies', that is, I was born in the sixties, the first of a working-class family. Apparently I was a miserable baby. This is vouched for by my mother and grandmother who tell me that, while we were living at my grandmother's house (my parents had to vacate their flat due to my arrival), I kept everyone awake at nights by crying. If I want proof I only have to look at a photograph of me then. I was taken to the photographers three times when my parents wanted to have my picture taken. Each time I started crying and was inconsolable so they left without one. On the third try I was given a toy dog to solace me and, although there are no tears, it is obvious that I am not very happy – to say the least. Maybe I was born miserable; anyway, I am glad that it no longer adorns the mantelpiece.

I do not remember these events of course, they are too far back, but some of my earliest memories are of primary school. I was popular with teachers and children alike, though I never felt inclined to play football at breaktime. I often took my toy cars in to race and still have the battle-scarred Porsche that was a winner on the playground tarmac. My mother bought this for me after my first dental filling. I was often treated to presents like that; she would let me choose a car, toy or Airfix kit when there was no special occasion. My mother got (and still gets) great pleasure out of giving and, when my brothers (born when I was two and five years old) and I were kids, she often went without herself so that we could have what we wanted. When I look back it seems miraculous how my parents managed to give us so much (especially at Christmas) when they had so little themselves. You don't see these things when you are young.

Back to school though . . . I suppose I was fairly clever. I never found any lesson particularly difficult, but I did not like sports. I enjoyed the challenge of maths, found science exciting, geography and history were interesting but art was the lesson I always looked forward to. Not that I can remember anything I did then. I tell a lie, there is one project I remember and it was not one that I did on my own. My best friend John and I decided to do a project together. The Tutankhamen artefacts being brought to the British Museum caused quite a stir and we were inspired to collage a full-scale copy of the death mask. We used a lovely book my grandparents had given me as reference. We used gold paper and metallic coloured foils to imitate the semiprecious stones; it was impressive by virtue of its size and we took it in turn to look after it after its completion. John and I also did a couple of academic projects together on 'Through the Microscope' which we were able to do because of the excellent microscope he had as a present — I kept those two exercise books for a long time too. . . . I cannot remember what happend to them. John used to visit my house on Saturday mornings and we would watch *Thunderbirds* together and I used to spend a lot of time at his house during the vacations. Although I got on well with my brothers in the house we rarely played together. At home I played a lot on my own and when I was not able to attend school due to asthma attacks I would draw pictures. Usually I copied colourful birds or wild animals out of the large animal encyclopaedia my parents gave me one Christmas. That was about all I had the energy for and I even found that difficult when I was ill. I remember just one occasion when I was so fed up with the attacks and the struggle it was to breathe that I said I wished I could just lay down and die.

There are a few things I remember about the house we lived in during my primary school years. We had a best/front room where my mother kept her record player. The house sported the colourful abstract wallpaper of the seventies and slot-together plastic lampshades. My father installed the bathroom suite which was a particularly nice shade of turquoise. The stairs were narrow and steep and on the landing my mother had pinned a newspaper cutting of a picture of Marc Bolan. I really liked T. Rex. I remember the first morning I heard 'Ride a White Swan' on the Tony Blackburn breakfast radio show. It stuck in my head and I was singing it to myself as I went into school that morning. However, there must have been something wrong with my perception because I could never manage to see Marc Bolan in the picture my mother had put up. Maybe it was too high and I was too short but I always saw a clown; this frustrated me somewhat. There was another colour poster of Marc in the front room which I could not mistake and my mother bought his singles of the time. I believe that it was this exposure which led him to be my idol.

Looking back I have tried to identify any early tendency to make myself unhappy but seem to remember only one incident. I believe it was my 10th (or 11th) birthday and I was expecting a birthday cake with candles on it. Instead I was presented with a selection of cakes. I can see now that my parents wanted to treat me more like an adult in recognition that I was growing up and my reaction still doesn't make much sense to me. I decided to get upset. Why? – to upset my parents! I really don't know, but my excuse was pathetic. There was a fancy cream slice which was obviously meant for me (being the birthday boy) and some other buns like Viennese fingers and doughnuts. I knew my mother liked Viennese fingers and the doughnuts were for everybody else. It is difficult to explain and probably doesn't make much sense but here is the reason I gave for my upset. I said the cream slice looked nice and I knew it was for me but, because I hadn't had one before, I didn't know if I would like it! I had had doughnuts before and knew I liked them. I should have wanted to eat the cream slice to show appreciation to my parents but instead I made a fuss and tearfully ate a doughnut. It is as if I was looking for a reason to spoil my birthday and have something to be unhappy about, as well as depriving myself of something I would like at the same time and my parents of some pleasure in giving. The odd thing is this has stuck fast in my memory and to this day I still feel uncomfortable about my birthdays and have a lot of difficulty in accepting gifts with the pleasure in which they ought to be received, almost as if I don't want to be happy and don't want people to try and make me happy. Silly really. My sister was born when I was eleven and we have always been pretty close.

During those years my father worked long hours and often weekends for a commercial transport company. In addition to the work involved in bringing up four children my mother also did typing at home to bring in extra money. I completed my first year of secondary education at an all-boys grammar school, the most memorable part of that being taking part in a production of *Oliver Twist* which my parents were unable to attend due to my father working late and my brothers and sister having to be looked after by my mother. My parents did not ignore my love of music, they paid for me to have clarinet lessons and I had ambitions to end up playing the saxophone, but we moved house and the new school did not have private music lessons. Scotland was where we moved and I attended my next two years of secondary education at a mixed comprehensive. Being the only English boy I was not very popular and when they knew I was leaving (because we were moving again) I had to dodge the gangs at the end of the day who wanted to give me a 'kicking in' as a leaving present. It was inevitable but fortunately I escaped unscathed except for a cut on my wrist where somebody's boot hit my watch and it cut me. I worked it out that, because there were so many of them (almost the whole school), no one was able to get a really good swing at me and I sort of swam my way through the sea of Dr Martens boots. Then ran like hell!

The final two years at school were thoroughly enjoyable, they were great, I was a legend in my lunchbreak! We moved to Surrey and I revelled in a sort of fame. I mean having lots of friends and being popular is a sort of fame and my paintings were often displayed around the school. I still remember the occasion when a younger pupil stopped me in a corridor to tell me how much he admired a particular painting. It was about the violence in Northern Ireland. Although I wasn't school prefect I was asked to join the house tutor and various captains and prefects for a Christmas treat – a Chinese meal out in a local restaurant. This was in recognition of the work I had done for the house in preparing posters for the various events like competitions and discotheques. I don't know when my interest in the 'East' actually started but it seems reasonable that it started then.

My mother agreed to perm my hair at home, which caused quite a stir among teachers and pupils alike, but it was the seventies and so I got away with it. I achieved good grades in all of my eight 'O' levels and my parents rewarded me by taking me to a music shop and letting me choose a second-hand guitar: something else no doubt that they could not really afford.

I never managed to get the hang of the guitar and that was my own fault through lack of dedication. Later I blamed the second-hand instrument but even upgrading to a new professional electric guitar when I had the money didn't help.

I put a lot of extra time into my artwork at school, often spending many extra hours at home in the evening and at weekends to try and produce work that was better than I could achieve in the space of the lessons. I always got good (if not the best) marks and took part with a few other 'top' pupils in an exhibition of work in the school hall during the vacation. Afterwards the tutors told me that several parents had wanted to purchase my pictures. I didn't want to sell them and still have them all. I had a very good relationship with my art teacher, he had a lot of faith in my abilities and when it came to the end of school he said to me to promise him that I would go into 'graphics' because he believed I would be very good in that field. I said I would but that was only lip service because as soon as school finished I was only interested in one thing – earning money.

Another fact that cannot be ignored is that my last year at school, 1977, was the year that Marc Bolan died in a car crash. When I went out I wore black in mourning for about three weeks. My friends, and their parents, must have thought I was very odd indeed.

I left school at seventeen and sought employment at Heathrow airport because it was so big anybody could get a job there. My first jobs were not very prestigious. I started as filing clerk but soon started moving up the ladder. Nevertheless I missed the recognition I had known at school – I was not noticed, and this was probably what prompted me to do more to make myself stand out. I started imitating my idol in more depth. I went to his tailor and had copies of his stage clothes made and had my permed hair dyed dark brown to match his. Where did I go looking like this you might wonder. Well, not shopping in the high street on a Saturday or round to friends' and relatives' houses for a start. On those occasions I was myself as I had always been, but there were enough occasions to go out looking like a pop star to warrant the expense. There were Marc Bolan conventions and a cinema in Dean Street screened Marc Bolan's film *Born to Boogie* every month. As far as I remember, I was still only imitating appearances at this time but I used to get a great kick out of other fans coming up to me and asking where I had got the clothes from or, even better, asking to have their photograph taken with me.

At the age of nineteen I suffered an almost debilitating disease, ulcerative colitis, leaving me unable to work for eighteen months. Losing my job was the least of my problems. My idol was never ill (as far as I knew), he was above such mundane experiences. The illness was a terrible blow to me, it was the most damning proof that I really was just an ordinary person. And what was the point of looking good if I was not well enough to go out? I was in pain most of the time and I remember that at the end of the day, when I was unable to sleep because of the pain, I often prayed that I might die in my sleep to save myself from going through another day of agony. I remembered some Chinese philosophy about the oak and the reed which made me consider this: if the pain was of a bodily origin then, if I could somehow detach myself from my body, I could avoid the sensation; if I could just let the pain flow through and out as it would, this might be less painful than trying to resist it. The various tests and examinations were humiliating and the best way to cope with them was to become detached from the situation, from the body. Ulcerative colitis was the final diagnosis and because of its advanced state surgery was suggested. When I heard that this would mean a colostomy bag I thought I would rather die. However steroids were an alternative, though the high dose made my face swell up like a football. My skin also suffered from the medication and I lost interest in my appearance.

After eighteen months I had recovered enough to get a job again, though not one that was physically demanding as my health was still fragile. Pure luck found me in the fashion business and this helped me to fuel my desire to be famous once again. I became quite well known in the trade and enjoyed being on the stand at the trade shows, being introduced to people as the designer. I could be as eccentric and flamboyant as I liked, it was almost expected of me. The perks of the job were pretty good too. I could have any clothes I desired made up especially for me. A bleached blonde bob and make-up were the only extra I needed to imitate the idol I had chosen this time. I did not feel like the person I was before I was ill, I felt as if I had been a fizzy drink that had had the cap left off and I had lost all my fizz. My new idol was more reserved, quiet, melancholy, untouchable, aloof. I decided I was never going to be ill again because I was not going to be ordinary. I detested the ordinary and I detested myself for my weakness, and lack of good looks – which the use of make-up did something to help.

I scoured the newsagents' shelves every week for photographs – so I could match my hair and clothes – and interviews – to find out what cologne he wore, what brand of make-up, what books he read, what other music he listened to. And all these things I acquired. Previously I read science fiction/science fantasy and would never have looked at the 'classics', let alone read them, or dreamed of buying Italian shoes and silk ties. Soon my whole world revolved around the perpetuation of this image, I imitated his manner of speech, the way he sat, walked. . . . I would not say that I was depressed, more that I was obsessed, obsessed with being someone else.

HOW I GOT INTO ART THERAPY

I had been very unhappy for a long time, the result of many seemingly unsurmountable problems all occurring within a relatively short space of time.

On the advice of a friend, and partly to please her, I stopped pretending to be something that I was not. For about 6–7 years I had been concentrating all my efforts, every minute of every day impersonating my idols, usually 'pop stars'. I had never been unpopular, but I just didn't like myself very much, I wanted to be someone special not an ordinary person like everyone else.

I was able to perpetuate these images through a large disposable income and my life revolved around perfecting these characters and continually updating them. When I disposed of this 'pop star' image I lost several things:
1. My own sense of identity. I did not recognise the person who looked back at me from the mirror. Not only was he a stranger to me but I did not like the way he looked either, he was very ordinary by comparison to what had been before and could have been anybody.

My friend tried to help me find a sense of self through taking a part in fashion but nothing I tried on in the shops felt right as I had always dressed to imitate somebody else, consequently I lost interest in my appearance.
2. I had lost my direction in life. My sole purpose of being had been 'to be someone else', someone famous, whom everybody liked, and now I was no one.

Over the years I had rejected my own personality in favour of those of my idols and, when I discarded theirs, I found I had nothing left. It literally felt as if I contained a vacuum, there was nothing I wanted to do.
3. Not only was my confidence crushed from the above things but also, by rejecting those interests that were a part of my other characters, I found I had no interests of my own and therefore nothing that would be of any interest to anybody else.

I felt as if I was a nobody with no character or individuality, indeed with nothing at all to offer anybody either by way of attractive appearance or interesting conversation. Hence I avoided socialising if at all possible and when I couldn't avoid it found myself trying to hide so that nobody would talk to me. I felt extremely vulnerable, even naked, that I no longer had a mask to present to people. I found socialising without any image very difficult. I felt as if I was presenting my naked soul to people. This made me very nervous and upset and I couldn't understand why everbody else didn't find it a problem to be themselves (even revelling in it) when they were nothing special either.

I became ashamed of myself and sick of never having any 'good news' for people, only my wretchedness, and this stopped me from even seeing people whom I knew to be friends of mine. My pride was also a problem here because how could I, who was known for being so flamboyant and always having something interesting to say, admit that he was really nothing at all except a very miserable ordinary person? I couldn't do it, and in that way cut myself off from one line of help many people would have used.

I started 'smoking' and found this was a very good way of wasting away those painful isolated evenings but it wasn't long before I fell into the rut of having to smoke myself to sleep every night.

My lack of interest in my own life reflected upon my work which, to be quite honest, by then meant nothing to me at all except for paying the rent. My boss obviously thought I should have been more company minded and consequently I lost my job.

At the same time as I was not struggling to keep the large rented accommodation I had, a previous business investment was going down the drain, and all I could do (all I felt I could do) was sit by and watch. By now I was taking it for granted that nothing would ever go right for me, it was my fate to be unlucky, so I complacently accepted these blows and just waited for the next disappointment.

After so many things going wrong I decided to start again. Indeed, it was all I felt I was capable of because I did not have the confidence or ambition to go on from where I was. I decided to return to college, to study in an area related to art. I knew I could never be an artist, but maybe I could be a designer, and still enjoy my work. That was the most important thing, to try and recapture the enjoyment I remembered from my school days. That was my dream, to enjoy my work as much as I had school because I now saw work as something I *had* to do, but did not enjoy, and thus I felt I was also wasting my life.

I did not succeed in getting a college place, but, as I could think of nothing else to do, I decided to 'take a year out' and prepare my portfolio in the hope I would secure a place the following year. This was going to be the toughest year of my life, but only because I made it so.

I found a 9 to 5 job, that would give me some free time to work on my art as well as keep my independence. It was an extremely tiring existence, I worked in the shop during the day and worked on my art in the evenings, often into the early hours of the morning in order to meet the deadlines I was setting myself to ensure progress. Saturdays were the same and on Sundays I was able to spend the whole day drawing and painting, I wouldn't allow myself to go out, my work was so important. I couldn't screw up getting a college place, it was my last chance and, therefore, I couldn't expect to be able to enjoy myself. Over the months I became extremely unhappy, basically because there was no enjoyment in my life, though I did manage to extract some happiness from a picture that went well. When a picture went badly however, it was hell, and this started a downward spiral which took all pleasure out of drawing and painting and consequently affected my output. I became sluggish in the execution. This slowness meant I had to spend more hours at it and often as I worked into the early hours I reflected upon the severity of my punishment, and concluded it was what I deserved.

I accepted that I had to work in the day, in order to have somewhere to work in the evenings, and I managed to get through the working day by role-playing the 'shop manager'; after all, I still had no character to present people with. In this respect things hadn't really changed much: instead of presenting people with a pop-star image I was presenting them with something equally unreal, the stereotype they expected to see, a blank card.

This hermit-like existence did nothing to help me rediscover my original character or rebuild my confidence. Eventually I became overwhelmed by such great sadness that, in the privacy of my own flat, I couldn't stop myself from crying. I usually felt better afterwards though, so I began not to mind it so much, and even to accept it as a necessary part of being able to get along this path I had chosen. It wasn't very long before this work-orientated life, with no rewards, made me very wretched and had worn down my hope of being good enough to get a college place and, if I couldn't get into college to start rebuilding my life again, why didn't I just put myself out of this misery and suffering and end it all? When I started thinking about suicide I realised it was time to ask someone for help. No way I could think of avoided the problem of a body, or the remains of it, which somebody would have to identify and I didn't want to involve any of my family (especially my younger sister and brother who had always looked up to me) or friends in such gory business. I imagined a machine that you could just step into, press a button and instantly vanish, just disappear! No pain, no mess.

At the back of my mind something was niggling me, the memory of how I used to be before I forgot about being myself and started being other people. In the midst of my wretchednes I could still remember a time when I was myself, quite a funny guy in fact. I had been suppressing my sense of humour for so many years now because 'smooth guys didn't tell jokes' that I felt I was no longer funny, but I wanted to get back to being the way I was so badly that I asked my GP if I could see a therapist.

I explained to him how unhappy I was, and the many reasons why, and that I had come for help to get back to being the way I was. I told him of my thoughts of suicide and how I had become detached from my body, how I loathed its appearance, inadequacies, and lack of skills, need for rest and the way I felt it to be a prison which carried 'me' around in it. How I felt I could do away with that body, after all, it would only be the end of my body, NOT ME.

I did not find this therapist of much use. He used to sit there and let me talk. This was the first person I had actually told all of my problems to and all I got were Freudian theories. I felt insulted, how could I be a text-book case?

Surely there was no one as sad as I was, I felt so wretched and awful, my case was unique. Who else could have impersonated pop stars so well for so long? I didn't like this very much. He seemed to think he was cleverer than me to be able to classify me, and, then, how could I let him help me? It would be another admission of my ordinariness. I started to cling to my awful wretchedness and misery because I felt it was that alone that made me different from everybody else. It was all I had that made me unique, it was all I was and I couldn't give it up.

I started playing a sort of game with him, being selective about what I told him (though I never lied) to make him draw a wrong conclusion. Perhaps this little game had something to do with ego.

My obsession with painting and drawing came up as a result of his asking why I didn't go out. He suggested I bring a couple of pieces and after this he suggested the possibility of art therapy and gave me a contact number. I phoned for an appointment and was asked to fill in a form being sent through the post. By now every day was such a great struggle. I knew I had been strong to have gone so far but I did not know how much longer I could go on fighting this battle on my own. I felt as if it took all my energy just to carry on living with nothing left with which to fight; every minute of my day was spent trying to defend myself from terrible feelings of doom and it was getting harder and harder to put on a brave face to anybody. I wanted help so badly that to ensure my application was not turned down I filled out the form in such a way to make it sound as though I was really desperate.

In retrospect I can see that I wasn't exaggerating, it was that I was so far gone that I didn't realise it myself.

REFERRAL TO THE CLINIC

Kim was referred to the clinic for art therapy by a psychotherapist who had been seeing Kim on a fortnightly basis for a period of six months. He had felt that words alone were not helping to uncover Kim's defence structures and help him express and explore his difficulties. Having seen a picture of his at one of the sessions, the therapist became aware that this was a more natural form of communication for Kim. It seems that Kim was very ambivalent about seeing another therapist, because of his uncertainty about its usefulness. At the first therapist's suggestion of seeing an art therapist, he became suspicious, declaring that he did not see a use for making art other than preparing material for his portfolio and getting into college. He could not imagine pictures having any other use. He was torn between feeling desperate and therefore the need to do something and his cynicism about his experience of therapy.

However, Kim followed up the suggestion of contacting the clinic and Gabrielle offered him an assessment interview, a procedure always followed prior to entering any therapeutic contract. He was asked to fill in an assessment form which gave details of personal history. He was also asked to describe the nature of his difficulties, experience of any previous treatment or physical ill-health.

DETAILS OF THE FORM THAT KIM FILLED OUT ON REFERRAL TO CLINIC

Please describe the nature of your difficulties, mentioning how long you have had them and your present condition.

From the age of 17 I have pretended to be someone else, usually a pop star and spent all my spare money on the upkeep of an image ie clothes made by tailors to these people, hairdo's at the same salons, make-up, flash cars, etc. Most relationships that developed were due to the fact that the young ladies idolised the particular artist I was copying at the time. That was until I met Sam who persuaded me to try and be myself instead. This had not been successful. The last couple of years has been hell. I do not like who I am and have felt suicidal at times through the depression caused through having to live with someone you hate (yourself). At the moment I am on the verge of slipping into another image to try and avoid another awful low. These are unbearable as I am prone to breaking down and crying for no reason apart from the fact that I feel so alone and that no one understands me.
In what way do your difficulties affect your life generally at the present time?
Because I do not like myself I find it extremely difficult to socialise. I feel so much less of a person than everybody I see around me (who seem to be happy with who they are).
What aspects of your life give you satisfaction?
For the last couple of years I cannot think of anything that has brought me any pleasure. Things that people tell me I should be pleased about do not give me pleasure because they always fall short of my expectations.
Please tell us something about your family.
Our parents have often argued and fought, my mother started divorce proceedings but my father was able to talk her out of going through with it. Their relationship has continued to deteriorate since. The family had attended family therapy for a short time because of concern over my sister who was suffering from an eating disorder.
In what way do you expect treatment to help you?
I must find a way of living with myself.

ASSESSMENT INTERVIEW AND THERAPIST'S FIRST IMPRESSIONS

Kim's story was to emerge slowly. I did not, on our first meeting, take a detailed history of his experience. I had the assessment form that Kim had filled in, but I wished to give Kim the opportunity for the pictures to emerge before the words. I felt that Kim had recounted a description of his life which it seemed he had told before. I hoped that, by the making of pictures, something new and fresh would emerge.

Kim sat on the edge of his chair. He sat there tense and rigid, his face blank and expressionless. He was immaculately dressed in a brown striped suit, black shirt and sombre tie with white shoes. His trousers were carefully pressed, his hair carefully cut and groomed. When he spoke his voice was flat and a monotone. He seemed suspicious of me but at the same time communicated a desperation. He quickly informed me that he could not see the point of coming to therapy. He was making pictures for his portfolio to get into college. He could not see that there would be any other purpose. He told me he had been rejected from college the previous year. He was now working on his own trying to complete a portfolio for interviews this year. He told me he would often go for days without seeing anybody. His work schedule was erratic, and he would often work late into the night. He looked tired, drained and flat. He was keen to tell me that, although therapy had been some help, he had not felt comfortable with the previous therapist. He had felt interpreted by him, and acknowledged that he had frequently felt in competition with him and that mind games were being played. He would select what he shared of himself with him. No doubt, Kim was trying to tell me at this point that he intended to do the same with me.

In spite of Kim's somewhat prickly façade, it was not difficult to see that, beneath his brittleness, there was a great deal of vulnerability. There was a very unhappy young man, caught between telling me that he was probably not 'sick enough' to come and see me and did not need help and a very desperate individual seeking help. He told me that he was sure that I saw people in much greater need than himself and that I should not waste my time on him. In spite of his protest, it was clear that he was testing my reaction in his attempt to see my response, transferring his expectation of being rejected. I was well aware of this pattern in new clients being seen at the clinic. The internal feeling of 'worthlessness' and 'not being entitled' to treatment could easily be misread as their ambivalence and suspiciousness. Most commonly underneath the surface is the fear that they will not be accepted and therefore the best form of defence is not to allow oneself to become involved for fear of rejection.

Kim, in his communication to me, was trying to cover up the pain of his own feelings of desperation. When I was able to share with Kim that I'd wondered if he had felt very frightened about coming and was worried about whether he might be accepted, he seemed to relax. I was also able to address his fears about his entitlement and him not seeing himself as worthy of time and space. I saw my task at this stage to reach out and try and make a connection with Kim's experience. I knew at this point that Kim did not have a language to describe his distress. One of the reasons that he was in such great torment was that he had a range of conflicting and confusing emotions that he did not know how to make sense of. In my first contact with him I had to function as a bridge between his internal chaos and the relationship we were to establish. I got some sense of how the defences he was presenting were on the surface. He was desperately calling out for someone to see below the surface of his communication. I asked Kim how he came to be here. He described a picture of an unhappy family. He told me his sister had been in treatment for an eating disorder. The family had been involved in family therapy. His parents had had a poor relationship for as long as he could remember. They had made attempts to separate but it had never happened. I had a picture of a family with a great number of tensions but with little communication. Unhappiness, withdrawal, misunderstanding and conflict were expressed with symptoms. Kim's own symptom was depression, withdrawal and suicidal thoughts. Underneath was someone who felt worthless, empty and without an authentic voice for his experience. Behind his protests was someone reaching out to be helped.

Context

While recognising our therapeutic concern to understand Kim's internal world expressed through his words and his pictures, it felt important for me to understand his experience of the world outside and the impact this may have had on his development. Growing up surrounded by images, particularly of a pop culture, must have profoundly influenced his perception of the world and how he saw himself. It seemed that Kim was heavily affected by a culture that valued façade and external presentation. In this type of culture, there is idealisation of and identification with popular figures. We project onto these people parts of ourselves that we feel unable to own for ourselves, both good and bad. They represent unavailable power and influence when we feel particularly powerless. They can represent intolerable bits of our own behaviour which we do not wish to acknowledge as our own. But these figures are created as unreachable and we do not wish to see them as real people with a complex set of emotions and ambivalent feelings. Kim had become trapped with a false persona.

Early on in our lives, we are taught to displace our own confusions, frustrations and often conflicting feelings. It is safer to externalise them and become consumed by heroes and villains of the day. It is the confusion of our internal lives that we do not feel equipped to manage which leads us to search for these representations. This serves to further alienate us from our true selves.

On meeting Kim I felt it was necessary to hold in mind the wider matrix. Kim had found and become part of a culture that was taken up with impressing the outside world. What was critical in Kim's case, and what led to his crisis, was the extent to which Kim became consumed by this all-pervasive activity. For Kim it had become elaborate and artificial, but provided meaning for his existence. When the façade began to disintegrate, it left him feeling empty inside and preoccupied by suicidal thoughts. The degree to which he had become obsessed suggested an unhealthy and destructive pattern of behaviour. My task was to help him make sense of his inner and outer worlds.

Therapeutic contract

After this first meeting we established a contract that we would meet on a weekly basis at a time that was agreeable to both of us. Kim agreed to this arrangement, although at the time it felt as though he did not have much faith in what this would offer him and how it might be of help to him. I outlined the time and day of our first session and said we would meet again then. His mood remained flat and expressionless.

Figure 1 Early image.

Chapter 4

Early image

KIM'S FIRST EXPERIENCE OF ART THERAPY: THE FIRST SESSIONS AT PARKSIDE

Even though I did not understand what art therapy was or how it could help me I could not avoid placing my remaining hope on it.

For the first session I purposely took no art materials or old pictures with me, I needed to be able to talk about the therapy first. I was feeling vulnerable and weak and did not want to have to deal with any surprises. I needed to feel as if I had some control over the situation. On entering the room however, the first things I noticed were the desk and the drawing materials. I remarked to Gabrielle that I would rather start the next time I visited. The second thing I noticed was the window. It was only a small window but because the room was a floor or two up the view was of the sky: a big blue sky with white clouds and the tops of trees visible. For some reason I always preferred windows with this outlook – a view that did not show buildings and people, that did not show the world and all the things in it. This view gave me a sense of freedom and tranquillity, perhaps it was more my ideal.

The third thing I noticed was the pictures on the wall; there were only a couple. One was a drawing of a strongman holding a pair of dumb-bells above his head. I didn't really understand what it meant and it was a cartoon-like drawing. The other picture however intrigued me. A woman's face with closed eyes and dark brown hair was profiled against a sky that was dark purple, blue and black. Lines had been scratched into the crayon that made up the sky and a big crescent moon hung facing the woman. The overall image and the fact it was executed in crayons (which I had always considered to be a child's medium yet this was a good picture) made quite an impression on me. I wondered if I would be able to do anything of a similar standard and felt slightly intimidated by it at the same time as being impressed.

I felt more comfortable in the presence of a female therapist. Gabrielle did not evoke the hostile feeling I had felt towards the previous male therapist. There was not the ego problem I had experienced before and I felt less embarrassed about telling Gabrielle of my terrible unhappiness. I felt I could lower my guard without loss of face. I remember being upset and tearful while telling her about how bad I felt; it was a great relief not to have to hide my sadness as I had to do when going through the daily routine.

Gabrielle's appearance differed greatly from that of my first therapist. His clothes were informal, he wore casual shirts, corduroy trousers, loud socks and casual shoes. Gabrielle on the other hand was very together, her appearance was very exact, her clothes were co-ordinated from head to toe and appropriate jewellery was also part of her look. I had always considered appearance to be of great importance and my impression of Gabrielle was that she was highly qualified in her field and that had to be respected.

Gabrielle explained that in art therapy I would illustrate (draw) my problems and then we would look at them together and discuss them. I still did not understand how this would be of help but Gabrielle's sincerity in wanting to help me reinforced my hope. I left with some comfort in the knowledge I had been accepted for treatment even though I was anxious about what I was going to do. What if my pictures were so bad that they would be of no use? Would I actually be able to draw something when asked?

I approached the second session with more anxiety than the first. I felt daunted by the prospect of drawing in front of somebody. Gabrielle asked me to draw about the way I felt. I wanted to show the extent of how sad and unhappy I was, and also impress her with a good picture to ensure future sessions. Unfortunately I could bring nothing to mind, and did not have the confidence to be spontaneous, so I duplicated an image I had made for myself three months previous. It was a silhouette self-portrait in sickly green, with bars (like prison windows) floating over the eyes, ears and mouth representing how I felt cut off from the world, and a hand (my hand) held a dagger threateningly above the heart (my thoughts of suicide). I was not happy with the way it turned out, I was nervous and I felt as if I was cheating. Perhaps if I had been more honest it would have been a better picture.

We discussed the picture but it did not yield much. I was not surprised knowing that it had been contrived. I knew Gabrielle saw through this charade but she was gracious and suggested that I should sign it. I had never put my name on any of my work, I never thought anything I did was good enough. Also what was the point of putting on the name of a nobody? Gabrielle also asked me to title it. I called it 'September' because my recent birthday had been the most painfully lonely time of my life and when I had started considering ending it all.

I left feeling disappointed, in myself, and resolved to approach the next session more honestly.

Although that first image was not much use in itself it did serve a purpose in helping me overcome my inhibition of drawing in someone else's presence. Gabrielle had not been critical of my foolish attempt to impress her. I was expecting a 'What do you think you are playing at?' remark but her patience in going through the process proved that she really did want to help me. This made me feel less anxious about the following session.

Gabrielle asked me to draw 'anything' this time. 'The way I used to be' cropped up often so I thought this would be an appropriate picture. I drew myself how I was ten years before, when I was happy to be myself at least some of the time. I am working on my favourite car, a very old Ford (no car was ever to take its place). I am wearing jeans and a lumberjack shirt and have long corkscrew hair. Casual dress was something I stopped wearing in favour of a more 'smooth' appearance when I started imitating my idols to extremes. As a restoration project I spent more time with my car than with friends. I know many people say they love their car, but more than that I could say it loved me back. Not only did I enjoy restoring it and showing it off, I felt the car itself was happy for me to drive it, the feeling was mutual. We had a great time, and it never let me down. When I lost that car in an accident I went through a period of mourning. My friends were scornful that I should be upset when I was lucky to be alive, yet I still felt I had lost something very precious to me . . . a friend?

People that came to know me since, cannot imagine that I would ever work on a car. Because of the images I took on, usually effeminate in some way, they had the impression I would never get my hands dirty.

This was such a poor quality drawing that I was truly embarrassed to put it forward for discussion. I was expecting Gabrielle to laugh at its childish naivety, but I did not see the slightest trace of amusement on her face. I was looking.

After having this first piece of honest work accepted I knew how to approach the future sessions. Gabrielle reminded me to sign it and I called it 'Kim'.

THERAPIST'S RESPONSE

Kim arrived 15 minutes late for our first meeting. I took him upstairs, up two flights of stairs to the art therapy room which is a very small box room. He seemed very tense and controlled. He sat on the edge of his chair and avoided any eye contact. The sadness in his eyes was very apparent but he seemed wary of me. His appearance was studied and immaculate, his hair was perfectly groomed. I was however struck by the rigidness of his presentation and there was a brittle quality to him. His voice was flat and without affect. He sat on the edge of his chair as he spoke and he quickly communicated that he wondered if art therapy could be of any use to him because he saw art as an intellectual exercise. He said he spent time at home making drawings to prepare for a portfolio to try and get accepted into art college. He could not see how painting could help him with his depression. He also communicated that he was sure that I probably had many people to see in much greater need of help than himself and he should probably not be wasting my time. Underneath Kim's words was a great deal of anxiety. I wondered to myself if he was worried that I might reject him as in some way being unsuitable for art therapy and unwittingly he was trying to protect himself against this. It is common for clients who are suffering from a sense of depletion and feeling worthless to consider they are not worth spending time on. I therefore suggested to Kim that he might be worried if he was going to be good enough or whether I might accept him.

I also decided to take some of the pressure off Kim at this point as his level of anxiety was so high. I therefore gently began to introduce some ideas of what I thought the therapy was about if we were to work together. I said we would meet together in this room for 50 minutes a session. It would be his time and for him to bring to the session what was important to him. I said a little about how he would have the opportunity of making images as a means of exploring some of his conflicts.

I am aware that the description of this process can make little sense to the potential client as it is necessary to experience the process before it has real meaning. The boundary issues have to be clarified in the first instance for the establishment of any therapeutic contract. Clients are often referred within the NHS with little or no idea of therapy or therapeutic process. I believe that the client has a right to know in what way one intends to work and to a degree what is expected of him. He also has a right to know in what way you are trained. The power relationship is a profoundly unequal one and this question can be interpreted as expressing the client's anxiety and a defence against this. My feeling is that this has the effect of disempowering the client. While recognising that working entirely in the transference may be a positive and creative process, being a blank screen in the early days can lead to 'persecutory anxieties' and intensify feelings of not being understood. In Kim's case, it seemed very important to reduce some of the tension in the room and make him feel a little more at ease. If he was feeling too anxious he would not be able to hear and take in what was being said. This also has to be balanced with the recognition that a degree of tension is important for change and growth. For Kim to feel sufficiently contained he needed to feel understood. In describing the process to Kim, I was taking some of the focus off him and thereby reducing his anxiety. By setting limits, it would act as a container for him. In communicating the structure and limits of the sessions, I was also indirectly reinforcing the time boundary. I chose not to pick up his lateness in this session as it was important to see if there was any pattern. He might also have experienced this as 'persecutory'.

I did however take it up in the subsequent session when he was again 15 minutes late. I acknowledged his difficulty in getting to see me and wondered whether there were practical reasons or whether he did not see himself as sufficiently 'worthy' and 'entitled' to the time to protect the space for himself. (Characteristically after this Kim always arrived early for the session and it would not be uncommon for him to arrive 30 minutes early.) The time boundary would always be held as it is part of the therapeutic task and part of the act of containment.

After I had set the limits Kim seemed to relax enough to start showing some of his despair. He described how awful he felt and how he would often spend days on end alone. While he was alone he sometimes felt sufficiently desperate to consider suicide. It would seem that his isolation had acted as some sort of magnifying glass that had led to the distortion of his mirror. He described how he didn't feel he had the energy to go on much longer. He had been trying to sort out his problems for years. He was now beginning to realise that, by avoiding them, his self absorption had turned all his thoughts and feelings inwards. In this isolated, cocooned world he was unable to remember that other people had thoughts and feelings. He was not however totally cut off as he seemed concerned whether I thought he was worth bothering with. He felt nobody wanted to spend time with him. He thought he was a drain on people and he had nothing to offer. When he was with old friends he said he felt paralysed and would dry up. His world was becoming totally inward looking.

In the early days of therapy, one of the strongest feelings the client will bring will be that of feeling misunderstood. Someone in great distress like Kim will probably have had many humiliating experiences of feeling his internal world is not understood. On the surface he might blame the world outside for being harsh and cruel and insensitive. Kim described this harsh world where he felt rejected, but, although he might have appeared to be blaming others, he had turned the real attack against himself in the form of depression. The task as therapist is to try and reach out and understand how he is seeing the world through his eyes. Once the client feels you have made this connection there is the possibility of establishing the foundations of a therapeutic alliance. Although the art materials were out in the first session, Kim was communicating that he did not feel ready to make an image. This seemed important to respect. To have precipitated this process before the client is ready and feels safe enough is likely to be counter-therapeutic. He was clearly testing me out and needed to lay other foundations before he started to draw. He was struggling with the question of whether I would be able to help him – would I be able to bear his awfulness?

Kim again talked of his previous experience of therapy which had been with a therapist with whom he had not felt understood; he had felt experimented and imposed upon with Freudian interpretations. He said that this therapist had suggested that he might be homosexual. Whatever the reality, the important issue is the all-pervading experience of being misunderstood and the anxiety that is conveyed about his fear of being 'experimented' upon in the same way. This also spoke to me about his fantasy that I would be no good either and again conveyed that the idea of making images had an absurd quality and he did not see how it would help him with his depression.

This anxiety is often demonstrated in the early session. The client has difficulty with the idea of making images. It is only the experience of the process that can clarify this and it is therefore not helpful to go into a detailed explanation which may merely serve to reinforce the client's defences. It was not until the next session that I gently but firmly invited Kim to make his first drawing. When I asked Kim to draw, he sat at the table with his back to me and I sat in one of the chairs. Many art therapists like to sit by the client so they can share the process. As the room was so small, this would have felt invasive, although I acknowledge it is also something about feelings about my own art process in that I feel inhibited and self-conscious when someone sits very close to me when I am trying to draw. It feels like an intrusion into my internal world. In a larger room, I feel there is more possibility for sitting next to the client, but in this instance I feel it was the appropriate response. A lot of the work developed into areas of how Kim felt overwhelmed by relationships to the point that he had little sense of who he was. I feel I was also responding to Kim's account of the intrusive therapist who had been so difficult for him. For Kim, to have fused with me so very early in the relationship would have been a very frightening experience and may have set up another negative transference.

The first image that Kim was to make was using paint. I had asked him to find a way of introducing himself to me on paper. He used soft greens and blood red and the marks were tentative. It was a self-portrait, with prison bars covering eyes, mouth and ears. Kim was communicating how isolated he felt and how disintegrated he felt his body was. There was a dagger piercing a heart. What came through was how difficult it had been for Kim to make an image because of his fear of me judging him. I was glad that he had made a start, that he had committed himself to paper in my presence. Perhaps in time it would not be so terrifying for him and he would feel safe enough to disclose himself honestly without so much fear.

In the next session Kim was to make an image that was to reveal a side of himself that as yet he had not revealed to me. He had shown me the highly anxious obsessive young man, immaculately turned out with an external façade that seemed impenetrable. Although unconsciously he had communicated his vulnerability, on the surface he had presented as brittle, trying to keep control, coming very close to the precipice and about to snap.

The image he drew was a young man bending over a car engine. (See 'Early image', Figure 1.) He is dressed in old jeans and a check shirt, his hair is wilder in appearance than that of the Kim in the room with me. In the background is a fence, with the gate closed. Kim has his back to me in the picture and he is tinkering with the engine. He described himself in this picture as the Kim that none of his friends saw and it was this identity that had been hidden by a number of masks that he had developed over the past ten years. The masks provided the identity that he showed to the outside world by dressing up as pop stars, imitating their dress, their personality, even their movements. He had a wardrobe that contained sequined jackets, velvet trousers and satin shirts, all imitating these pop stars. As he talked about when he used to go out, the real Kim no longer existed, I was getting a sense of the huge gaping hole it had left inside. This was becoming visible as this external suit of armour was breaking down. Kim had so obsessively developed these masks over the years that he had lost contact with the other side of himself. Kim seemed to relax towards the end of the session – perhaps relieved to show me and himself this other side and to discover it was not to be rejected. The image mirrored a genuine part of himself that he had kept so well hidden. The picture was neither immaculate nor perfect but a quick honest drawing.

OVERVIEW

Once the therapeutic contact is established, the first sessions are important as they clearly show the tentative initial stages of the therapeutic alliance. The treatment alliance can be described as:

> being based on the client's conscious or unconscious wish to co-operate and his readiness to accept the therapist's aid in overcoming internal difficulties. This is not the same as attending treatment simply on the basis of getting pleasure or some other form of gratification. In the treatment alliance there is an acceptance of the need to deal with internal problems, and to do analytic work in the face of internal or (particularly with children) external (e.g. family) resistance.
>
> (Sandler *et al.* 1973: 30)

First impressions, expectation and even some preconceptions might be at work in influencing the alliance and the fears and anxieties, expressed in different ways, are clearly described by both therapist and client. Three important variables inevitably influence the meeting of the client and therapist – what the client brings, what the therapist brings and the setting in which they meet. Each views the other through the eye of the past, which colours present expectations, and this forms the emotional impact of the client on the therapist and vice versa. This process is clear for us to see in these early sessions. The anxiety becomes focused on the making of images which is the unique aspect of the art psychotherapeutic process. Commitment to begin the therapeutic process has a physical basis in terms of actual attendance and an emotional one in terms of the decision to make use of the sessions. The lateness can be understood as one way of testing this out for the client and is common in the early stages of therapy. It raises questions in the client about how much he wants to come, how acceptable he will be to the therapist and is an expression of ambivalence about the undertaking of treatment.

This was described clearly in the therapist's notes. Her response to it demonstrates the importance of internal dialogue in the therapist's mind. The therapist holds in mind and thinks about process as she is working and remains available to the client's feelings and communications. The dialogue reminds herself of his experience while holding in mind the theoretical framework. Unless and until questions of dynamics and process are understood, the therapist will not be able to take these in later on.

This is illustrated by the title of this chapter and issues about 'Early image'. The process of these first few sessions raises thoughts about whether the 'image' refers to the self or the picture and immediately involves the 'image' of the therapist and client. These are clearly intertwined and the process of making the pictures in the sessions shows how Kim's low self-esteem was reflected in his anxiety about beginning to draw although he paradoxically stated that he did not think that 'art' could help him. He projected this anxiety onto the therapist by expecting her to laugh at him and his efforts at making images. Following the process closely from the beginning, it is important to note how much the surroundings in the room made an impact on him. Kim clearly describes his sense of vulnerability and need for points of contact and familiarity. His eyes are drawn to the window, the desk and the art materials – things that he feels most comfortable with – and then on to the paintings on the wall which confirms his sense of feeling intimidated and worthless. He uses these as a confirming experience, but does not articulate this at this stage and so it is not taken up directly except in the therapist's general first impressions of the client's response to the room.

The response to the images in the room can be worked with as part of the material of the session. There is some debate within the art therapy profession as to how much work should be hung on the walls of the therapy room and to what extent this affects the process of the treatment. From this description there is no doubt that pictures so displayed have an effect, and this can be useful. Sometimes material can be gleaned from comments about pictures in terms of understanding about what is being projected onto or identified with in the images. Some clients might find the images disturbing or distracting, or indeed may feel swamped by them. Using images in this way is all part of the material that the client brings to the sessions but it can be detrimental if the experience is so difficult that the client feels too daunted to function.

It is important to clarify that making images in a therapy session has a different purpose from art made for public exhibition in which aesthetic quality will be a major consideration in how it is received. The art process in a therapy setting is important in that the client can choose and it is in his or her control, the extent to which he or she chooses to emerge from that essentially private inner dialogue of the creative act. Schaverien emphasises this point:

> The artist who has finished her picture has now to consider where to show it. She may choose not to show it, keeping it private. It exists then as her private framed experience which perhaps feels too precious or powerful to risk showing. It may be a dialogue with herself, or something of which she is ashamed, or maybe she anticipates others' rejection of it. Quite possibly her motivations are unclear; it just feels wrong to show it. The client in therapy may well go through similar feelings in deciding whether to show her picture to the therapist. This transition from private to public is a common feature of all art. It is a step from the process of image making to acceptance of the picture as a product.
>
> (Schaverien 1989: 152)

Here we see immediately a new set of choices that are presented to the client in art therapy. The art product is different from the spoken word as an expression of feeling, and sensitivity about what happens to the final image is obviously important. Whether the image goes on the wall is therefore an important statement for both the client and the art therapist to make. As a general rule, if it feels useful that images are hung on the walls, their presence in the room reaffirms the sense that images are valued and are an important dimension of the work. As it is one of the tasks of the art therapist to look after the images safely and in confidence, if a client asks for a painting to be hung on the wall then this must be seen as part of the process of the session and any decision about this kept within the treatment context.

To return to Kim and his initial meeting with the art therapist, he noticed these aspects in the room before he felt able to acknowledge the presence of the therapist and allow himself to be aware of her impact. As we have already mentioned, both therapist and client will have strong feelings at this stage of the process – client wondering what will happen and the therapist wondering how and if the treatment alliance will be established. Any anxiety of the therapist's should not be conveyed to the client – she must be able to absorb and contain the client's intense difficulty and therefore this must not be blocked by the feelings of the therapist. This is clearly described by Kim's sense of being contained and understood without too many 'explanations'.

There is a big difference in terms of what is noticed and the 'impact' in the first meeting between therapist and client. Kim notices the images, but, as she is familiar with the room, the therapist notices the client and the way he is presenting himself. This provides clues for her, although at this stage there is no indication of the extent to which this is a 'charade', which is how Kim describes himself. Her response is free from this sort of judgement and her acceptance is perceived as holding hope. He begins to relate to her gradually, as we see from the text, and she manages to contain his anxiety without the need to be directive or describe too much about the process at this stage.

His anxiety about beginning is immediately transferred on to the therapist by being impressed by her 'togetherness' which is a projection based in his own sense of 'untogetherness'. The impact of her clothes is striking to him and here we see in the immediate transference some attempt at identification – seeking out in her something that feels familiar for him. This type of mental organisation or defence has the effect of holding himself together. The clothes he has chosen to wear have been a façade and yet he can still see his association of 'having control' in other people even though it does not work for him. One further point worth considering is that if the therapist is perceived as being so 'together', this may have a counter effect on the client who might perceive the gap between his experience and that which he is projecting on to the therapist as being too wide to enable the possibility of a therapeutic alliance. This might be one reason for a potential client declining the offer of therapeutic work.

In Kim's case, it was not off-putting – if anything, it had the opposite effect of enabling him to 'think' about this issue in a different way, made an immediate bond with the therapist and, as will be discussed, greatly influenced his first image. The effect of the 'image' of the therapist on the overall process can be seen to be as strong as the images on the wall.

It is interesting to note the extent to which the client on first meeting does notice the outward appearance of the therapist. Therapists should be aware of outward appearance and what effect this has on the development of transference. Fundamental issues such as race, colour and ethnicity need also to be considered as these too will affect the initial stages of the therapeutic relationship. For Kim the gender of the therapist was particularly important.

The sessions develop as Kim is able to produce an image, after quite some time as he needed to feel safe. He realised this was not an honest picture (like his own outward appearance) and this was quite important in terms of Kim's particular difficulties. It is worth noting that this is fairly common at the beginning of most art therapy relationships. The art therapy process often 'starts' with a safe, known image such as a well-worked-out cartoon, graffiti image, a doodle, as if there is a need to test out the safety of the space in which the person and now the image will be placed. It is like starting a conversation, such as commenting on the temperature or weather. This testing-out process is useful for art therapists to be aware of in terms of the different 'levels' of statement. All images are genuine personal statements but some might be superficial in that they are 'safer' images that are produced before the defences begin to be lowered and the inner feelings are allowed to come to the surface. However, as they always are personal statements, they are of equal importance and must be fully accepted. The analytic equivalent is that the client 'knows' that they are talking on a more superficial level and this may or may not necessarily be a conscious process.

Schaverien (1992) makes the distinction between the 'diagrammatic' and 'embodied' image. She describes the diagrammatic picture as that which is usually an approximation of a preconceived mental image. It is a linear reproduction of an image or a type of picture that is seen 'in the mind's eye'. This type of picture needs to be explained with words and, although this is conscious in intent, unconscious elements may be revealed. The feelings around may evoke affect but these are not attached to the picture itself. The diagrammatic picture is often controlled in its execution and often figurative and specific and, most importantly, is a result of a detached attitude to image making. This in turn runs parallel to the detachment in the therapeutic relationship and this resistance therefore becomes an aspect of the transference relationship. It is likely that, if the client is not engaged with the image-making process, then he is not engaged with the therapist as a person. This process is shown very clearly here. In the transference he had an expectation of humiliation and that the therapist would see his defence at this stage. He had empowered the therapist with all-seeing eyes. He felt the therapist knew that his picture was a charade in spite of the fact that she had made no indication about this. She valued it and this shows clearly the direct link between the way he values himself and his pictures – he felt strongly that the therapist could see what a charade his picture was and so therefore he was a charade. As this is his experience, the image is thus connected to the client as a personal statement. The complete acceptance by the therapist of both images again shows how his feeling of anxiety about being rejected was projected on to the therapist. He was sure she would reject 'such a poor drawing' but it was valued equally. We can now see and safely speculate how damaging it is to make judgemental comments about any work produced in art therapy whatever the circumstances.

Inhibition about image making is a common occurrence within an art therapy relationship. It usually conveys the message that the client feels 'not good enough' and the feeling that because the drawing is no good he is no good. It takes time and containment by the therapist to enable a safe enough space for the client to begin to make images and this is clearly described in the process. Making marks leaves a permanent record and therefore involves greater risk, as these aspects will be more indelible than the spoken word. This forms part of the process and a record for future reference.

For Kim it was an important turning point to make this commitment. He was presenting as a highly anxious, rather obsessive young man immaculately turned out, with an external persona that seemed impenetrable. Although he was clearly very vulnerable and brittle, he was trying to present as a young man in control but on the edge of becoming emotionally out of control. By waiting for the process to occur, for him to feel safe enough to begin to draw, the therapist was seen to be containing these anxieties and inhibitions and in this sense he could free himself from them. It is very important to wait for this moment when the client is ready to make the move into images which will cause some anxiety itself. Over-anxious art therapists might be easily led into prompting this process as they feel safer when images are being made since this is their 'language'. There is an equivalence to interrupting a silence in the analytic session; the art therapist should not be tempted to prompt prematurely the activity of image making.

The therapist worked with Kim's need to remain hidden but did not interpret this. Her feeling was that, if she made an interpretation too quickly, her comments would have felt invasive and the client would have felt the need to close off. There is a danger of premature interpretation and in this case there is always the question of why Kim chose to leave the previous therapist. Gabrielle describes how she chose to sit away from him waiting for this process and this was in response to her own feelings about invasion and the cues Kim was giving. The importance of this was in fact communicated in the image itself as the therapist describes him with his back to her – a detail of the understanding of the counter-transference response to Kim's struggle to engage. This immediately establishes an important dynamic between therapist and client based on projective identification. Kim's resistance resonates with the therapist's in terms of the understanding of her use of this defence in her own process. If there is toleration and respect for the defence, in this case the fear of invasion, then it becomes easier for it to dissolve as a barrier for work to begin. If the defence is attacked too quickly, this can be devastating and so there is a need to be vigilant in allowing the client to free his own process at his own speed.

It can be seen how useful this process was for Kim. He was allowed to begin in his own time after going through an important initial response and reflection on the therapeutic space that was being offered. By beginning to draw images, in a sense Kim was beginning to gather some sense of self-determination. He could say what he wanted in his own time and space and language in a voice with which he felt most comfortable and that, most importantly, he felt would be heard. By looking in his immediate area of experience, he could begin to think about his empty inner life which had for so long been unattended and neglected. It was as if the car is himself and at last someone is beginning to look under the bonnet and look at its engine, the internal works which are central to the functioning of the machine. Kim had not allowed anyone else to do it for him, and indeed had not allowed anyone else to see these aspects of himself, and so it was important that he should make these first moves himself. It was as if this image represented some statement about the fact that Kim was becoming able to open his own bonnet and begin, albeit tentatively, to look inside and examine the different aspects of self inside the shell that was presented to the outside world.

Having led a life of imitating pop stars in their dress, movements and personality, he had built up his outer shell which formed the basis of his social interaction to the point where he could function only with this mask or false persona. As this false identity developed, he denied himself an opportunity to develop his real self. This was to leave him hollow and empty inside. Gabrielle comments that she feels in touch with a huge gaping hole. Making the images began a discovery of who he was on the inside and there must have been some anxiety that there would be very little to discover – or, to continue the metaphor, that all the 'engine' would be rusty and useless and destined for the scrap-heap. Also, he was allowing some aspects of his inner self to be shared with another person – the therapist – which was a very important step in establishing the therapeutic alliance. He was skilled at keeping people at a distance through his words and false persona. Making the image provided him with an alternative, less threatening means of communicating his feelings and difficulties and thereby provided another voice which he could not so easily censor.

Much of this communication Kim was beginning to articulate but many of these aspects conveyed in his image remained unconscious at this stage. The cathartic nature of art begins the unfolding process at an unconscious level. This has the effect of beginning to release material that has previously been hidden and repressed. The presentation and discussion of the completed image was important to hold together the communication. To have explored how the picture evolved might have felt too intrusive but again was an indication of Kim's need to present the finished picture to the outside world. This process puts us in mind of Winnicott's theory of true and false self, as outlined in Chapter 2, which is based on the fear of discovery of the true self and the false self which serves to protect it (Winnicott 1960). We will need to hold these thoughts in mind as the therapy proceeds.

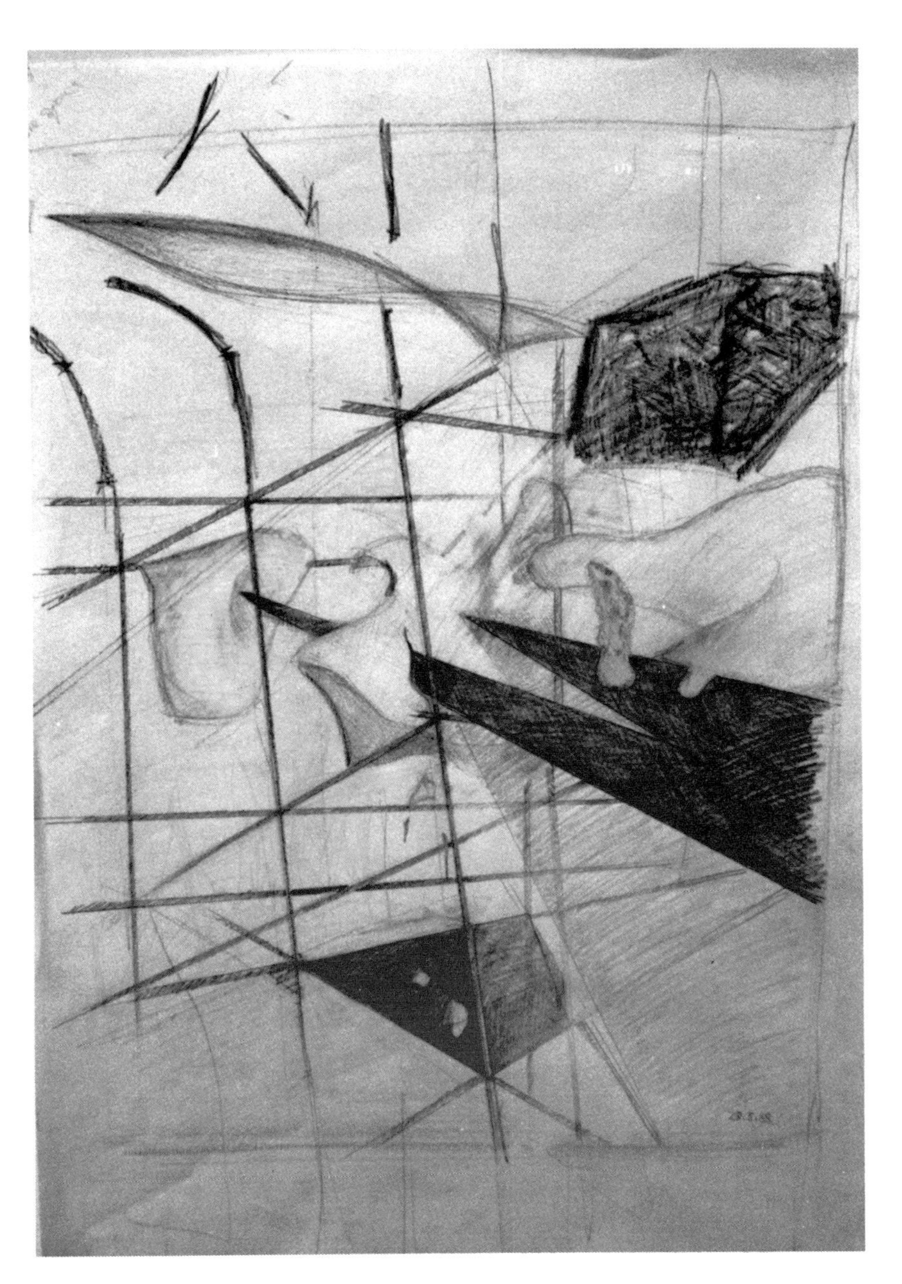

Figure 2 Trap.

Chapter 5

Family pictures

KIM'S FEELINGS, RESPONSES, MEMORIES

The tenancy of my flat expired, and, because I was hoping to secure a college place later that year, I decided to move back to my parents' house until I knew where I would be studying. This should have made my life easier, but it didn't. Being back at home meant that I had to fall in with the run of the house and was confronted with other problems, which in addition to my depression caused me further anguish.

I shared a bedroom with my brother who was still at home. There was no room to paint or draw in the bedroom but I was allowed to work in the living room, although not with any smelly or messy media. This limited what I could do and as the television was always on I found this a great distraction. I considered 'watching television' an ordinary thing to do and, because I did not want to be like other boring people, not owning one was a mark of my difference. Mealtimes punctuated my work too so my most profitable hours were from 11 pm to 2 am when the family were in bed.

My days off from work in the shop should have been time for me to work on my portfolio but my mother required much of my time as she felt she could not talk to anyone else in the family, that is that no one else would listen or care. I was and always had been the only one she could talk to. I would listen and try to give her some words of comfort or advice, but by this time I had nothing to give her. How could I be cheery for my mother when I felt so sad myself, or give her hope when I had none? I really felt that I could not cope, but I did the best I could because if I had turned my back on her she would have had no one. My parents' marriage had not been as it should for some years and often I found myself keeping the peace between them, trying to defuse awful rows, and, if not between them both, then between one of them and my brothers and sister. Because I had been the peacemaker in the past, it seemed that role fell to me again, but this time I noticed my reconciliatory skills were to the benefit of everybody except me.

The abstract images that I was doing at this time were an attempt to illustrate the pressure I felt I was under through being back at home. I felt like fabric being torn apart, wearing thin and my soul was showing – through my weakness I was losing the strength to carry on with my façade. I had barely enough strength to cope with my own depression and now I was being asked to support other people as well. It was unbearable. I felt I was breaking, cracking up or crumbling under the pressures and was also being caught in the crossfire of the various conflicts between the rest of my family.

In many respects I was fairly pleased with the graphic representations of how I felt because they were interesting to look at, but something about them frustrated me. They were too clean, too clinical to really express how awful the situation was and they lacked expression because I had thought of metaphors or symbolism that I could use rather than just trying to express it.

The family unit is represented by the framework which holds the various members. Being back at home felt like imprisonment, albeit self-imposed. Not everybody was a prisoner there though. My two brothers had escaped. One I represented by a bird shape breaking out of the top because he had recently left home and was doing all right. I had to comfort him because the family situation often upset him and I had helped him with his resolve to leave. The other is represented by a heavy square block because I did not know this one so well, but I could see how he did not let living at home affect him, he just did what he wanted to do, when he wanted to do it, and did not get involved in the arguments, even the ones that were about him. Perhaps I should have drawn a bulldozer.

I drew myself like a white ghostlike shape in the centre of it all. I am standing in front of my sister who is cornered by my mother. I am trying to protect her from the stabs (verbal not physical) my mother would make at her. I could not be around all the time and on more than one occasion of returning from work my sister would come to me crying because my mother had said something during the day to upset her. My father is represented by the green rounded shape. He was neither soft nor chubby, in fact he was strong due to the physical nature of his work, but, although he had reprimanded us when he was home, he was not at home often. The task of reprimanding us often fell to our mother and it was my father's duty to back her up when he came home from work, so there he is taking her side. My mother often stated that she felt she was the ogre because she always had to do the telling off and I felt sorry for her because she would so much have liked everything to run smoothly. And why shouldn't it have?

Nevertheless, when I did get involved in the family conflicts, I couldn't help feeling hurt myself. I wanted so much to be in a place where arguments never happened. I often felt as if I were being torn apart by having to take sides when really I didn't want to. The hurt I felt myself at these times is shown by the pieces of me which have been cut off in the conflict and are dropping into the pit at the bottom of the framework.

It was a painful situation to examine the family so closely. Gabrielle had asked me to do so, but I hadn't realised that it really was so much of a problem to me. Perhaps I didn't want to admit it to myself. It wasn't until I tried to draw it that I really thought about it and began to realise how awful life at home was. I felt embarrassed about bringing this picture to the session because I found the family situation embarrassing – most families I knew got along really well together, as a family should. I also felt a bit guilty about the way I portrayed my parents but that was how I felt. I was hoping Gabrielle wouldn't think that I was showing myself as some kind of martyr, though sometimes I did feel as if I was being crucified. A positive aspect of this picture was that this insight into the mechanics of the family unit made it a little easier to cope with.

THERAPIST'S RESPONSE

Once Kim began to make images he began to relax. The act of having his back to me as we sat together seemed to allow him to enter his private world and begin to release a side of himself that had been very tightly held in place. I was aware of Kim's fragility and brittleness and I felt the communication from Kim not to invade his space. I was to learn in time that this had special meaning for him as he was especially sensitive about experiences of feeling invaded or intruded upon.

Kim made a picture for about 20 minutes and then he brought it over to the armchair opposite me and we explored the image together. The sessions were 50 minutes long and, although this time boundary acted as a safe container for Kim, it also seemed to inhibit the depth to which he could develop his image. I therefore made the suggestion that Kim might want to make some pictures at home and bring them to the session. While recognising that his isolation had been a defence against having relationships in the outside world, he was also learning to use the private space to develop a part of himself. He had set up a punishing schedule for himself preparing his portfolio, and this had fed into his sense of worthlessness and left him feeling empty and drained. However, he did have the capacity to work alone, and, while in the long term I hoped that the presence of another would not make him feel invaded and overwhelmed, I recognised a resource that he already had. There was some internal structure amidst his chaos. Kim responded readily to my suggestion.

It is important that I was thinking of the consequences when introducing this extra dimension to the relationship. For some clients, to make images at home without the presence of the therapist is too uncontained an experience as it may catalyse some powerful material that may be overwhelming. For others there is a sense that they can hold the therapeutic relationship inside themselves which acts as a container. This occurs by the client providing a safety net which allows him to recreate an internal representation of the therapeutic encounter. This has the effect of intensifying the therapeutic process by introducing a more frequent therapeutic structure and brings an additional depth to the relationship as the client can reach a depth of self-expression not so available in the time of one session.

For Kim, although I sensed he felt very near the edge and making the images would stir up some powerful material, he seemed to have made a sufficiently powerful positive relationship in the transference to enable this and, because of his ability to use images, they would act as containers in themselves in holding himself together. I was also aware that there might be some pleasure for him in being able to communicate some of his genuine technical skill outside the session. It was clear that the time limitation was inhibiting his ability to communicate a part of him that was so clearly developed but had not been recognised. In the art therapy relationship one is never looking for technical competence or the ability to produce beautiful images. Sometimes it may be important for the client to communicate this. In the same way as verbal ability may lead to self-confidence, image agility can also lead to a sense of validation. Kim had been making pictures over the last year in a very isolated world. He had had nobody to 'mirror' his experience, to reflect against or in any way test his reality. His mirror had become distorted. By suggesting this I hoped that I was bringing his outside world into therapy and taking the therapy into his outside world.

Kim made this first family image in my presence but was to develop the theme outside the session into a very powerful and important series of drawings. It was at my suggestion that this first image was made because he was presenting material that suggested that he was deeply preoccupied by, entangled with and overwhelmed by his family at this stage and found these confused feelings extremely difficult to articulate verbally. Making images about it would be an attempt to untangle the web and also to facilitate some beginning of sharing his own experience and his feelings of being in his family.

He chose a symbolic way of representing his family (see 'Trap', Figure 2). In the picture Kim has drawn a grid which, on first impression, looks like barbed wire. The first image shape I saw in the picture was the sharp black pointed spear shape, which was cutting on the wings of the blue bird, and piercing into the softer orange heart shape. Kim described the spear shape as his mother, the blue bird was himself and the heart shape his sister. His father, he said, was the floppy green shape which was contingent on his mother. The blue fish shape which is at the top of the picture was one brother, the heavy black rectangular shape was the other. Kim has placed himself in the centre of the picture with the piercing sharp blades of his mother cutting under his wings. His father's faint and flaccid image is also resting on him and the bird is looking in the direction of his sister. He placed his brothers at some distance from the rest of the family as they, it transpired, had found ways of separating themselves.

The picture could be likened to a family sculpture in family therapy where it quickly demonstrates the patterns of communication. Kim was to tell his family story. Ever since he could remember, his parents had had a difficult relationship with very little communication between them. There was a great deal of blame and recrimination on his mother's part. He described her as angry and full of frustration and she would look to Kim for consolation. His parents had attempted to get divorced, but when it came to it they were unable to separate. He described his father as passive and his mother as unhappy and frustrated.

Each family member seems to have found a different way of handling the tension and unhappiness. His younger sister developed an eating disorder, his brothers distanced themselves from the family by finding other relationships outside the home. Kim often took on the role as mediator in the family. His mother turned to him for support and understanding. She would expect him to understand her world and her experience. Kim felt there was little room for his needs and development. He was expected to be the parent for her and so there was no parent for him to act as a container for his feelings which would allow him to mature emotionally.

As a result, over the years, although he gave the impression of being able to respond, he described how he developed his suit of armour, a pretence whereby he did not have to think and feel but could keep the world out. This it would seem linked with the foundation of his depression, where he stopped himself feeling and became shut off with feelings of emptiness. Neither parent was available to or able to understand their children's experience. They would seem to have been too caught up in their own emotions and preoccupations. Kim's father used the defensive mechanism of withdrawal while his mother would swamp him with her uncontained feelings. Kim therefore had little experience of feeling understood, as the parents had no space for the children's emotional needs. The development of symptoms in the children can be understood to be a means of communicating their distress. Kim's depression and suicidal thoughts would seem to be connected to his feeling of being unable to communicate and be understood.

As he was able to share this experience of his family, it was essential to be able to bear his pain so that he could feel understood and that he could see that I was not overwhelmed by his despair as his parents had been. As he became involved in the picture making, he began to feel some of the pain of living in his family. His 'suit of armour' was holding less tightly intact and he was beginning to experience some of the distress that he had repressed for so long. By taking off this protection, his sense of vulnerability was temporarily increased, but by letting go of some of his defences and exploring his feelings he would have a genuine opportunity to discover his own potential for creativity. He was also to be allowed to let go of his false self, i.e. his suit of armour, and in the therapeutic relationship allow himself the space to experience his true feelings.

Kim felt enormous despair after he had produced this picture. He had entered therapy hoping to experience some relief and feel better. He had managed to survive before by sealing off any emotions, his feelings had been frozen. The act of entering therapy and the process of making these powerful pictures meant that there was no relief but greater pain for him at this point. To learn to live with these feelings was frightening for him. The image, however, was to communicate a part of Kim which was still hidden and unknown to him. I was able to see that, while the points of the sharp sword might be piercing the wings, they may go under the wings of the bird, giving potential for flight and possible escape. The grid reminded me of barbed wire and I wondered if for him it represented something dangerous, life-threatening and persecutory. While clearly it continued to have this meaning, it may also be seen as a container, as an attempt to give order and meaning to his world, some psychic space.

I shared these observations with Kim. It meant nothing to him at the time and he was unable to take it in. His overwhelming feeling was one of despair. He was not ready to observe that there might be a flight path out. Although Kim was not ready to internalise the belief that there were other alternatives, it did allow me to contain for him this possibility. I would hand this back to Kim when he was ready to take it in for himself but, in the meantime, it was my task to hold the hope for him. I was, however, available to help him tolerate his despair and to be able to communicate my belief that he could survive this. I was to do this by explaining that some of the distressing and frightening emotions were being churned up because he was allowing the therapy to touch him and this was the beginnings of the process of change. He was showing some of the first signs of allowing himself to have feelings. He had firmly established the foundations of a therapeutic relationship.

OVERVIEW

What is striking about these sessions is how quickly the important material is coming to the surface and the responses that are made to this by both therapist and client. To some extent Kim has begun the painful process of symbolically 'opening his bonnet' which seemed to unleash a depth of feeling of being overwhelmed and entangled. But we must bear in mind that this was partially a transference response to the therapist – in describing the emotional burdens of his mother, perhaps this was the expression of his fears about the therapist: was she going to be a burden and was he going to become ensnared by her? Gabrielle had required him to be on time and had suggested that he begin to draw and use the images to express his feelings about the family. Was Kim seeing Gabrielle as the demanding mother or pulling her into that role as his response to women in authority? How did it feel for the therapist when the client so clearly described his experience of being merged, with very little sense of who he was?

These are important questions to bear in mind, as there are two active interventions by the therapist which have a significant effect on the process of the sessions. Firstly, she suggests to him that it is possible to make images outside the session and bring them as part of the material to be used. Gabrielle explains her thinking behind this and this adds another dimension to the process of further work. But it is always useful for us to think about why this might have occurred at this stage and there may be some pointers in the counter-transference response that show these unconscious processes at work.

In the early sessions there had been an identification in terms of feelings of invasion. It was difficult to sit too near Kim as this was experienced as potentially intrusive. Perhaps the suggestion to work at home was linked with this – to allow Kim as much space (and time) as he wanted to make his images, to enable him to use these positive aspects of himself. The therapist was holding in mind his ability to produce images for himself, but interestingly was not aware at this stage that Kim felt that his initial attempts had been a 'charade'. The therapist had seen an evolution into more honest, genuine image making and much less anxiety in the process of making them. Gabrielle felt able to suggest this to Kim through her own counter-transference response, as she knew the value of this way of working through an understanding of her own processes. Her own need for space and privacy, to find a private creative world that is separate and outside the influence of another, and then to have the experience of another person's response to it through the language of the image, was central to her understanding of Kim's needs at this point.

This response seems to provide an important bridge in their relationship and was also a response to Kim's more direct communications. His fears of invasion and intrusion were directly expressed in his experience of the first therapist, and became manifest in the transference itself, and this was further clarified in his subsequent description of his invasive mother. One important indicator for us to think about is that it was the sharp point, which was later described as symbolising his mother, that was first noticed by the therapist. This indicates how visually the images are powerful, as this response to the image informs the therapist of the unconscious communications. Gabrielle had also responded to her sense of the 'gaping hole' in the previous session. Was she thinking that she might get 'sucked into this'? Her awareness of the lack of time for image making in the session might have connected with some anxiety about the intensity of the communications that were being expressed. By extending the matrix, there is a mutual feeling that both therapist and client will have time and space to work more effectively.

Let us consider briefly this way of working in art therapy. Suggesting that work can be done outside the session time and brought to the sessions has the effect of extending the matrix. Some art therapists work only with the image that is produced during the time of the session and in the presence of the therapist. This enables much more focus on the process of creating the image, the order in which aspects of the image are put on the paper, the mood and feelings generated by this activity and the countertransference response of the therapist to the image and painting client. Other art therapists accept that time limitations of the actual session can be a restraint and, if images are made outside the session, the therapist is willing to look at these as part of the material. This shifts the dynamics as the boundaries are changed to incorporate time outside the actual session time. One way of looking at this is that dreams, dreamt outside the time of the session, are brought to analysis and form an essential part of the process of understanding unconscious material. Pictures contain unconscious material and can therefore be brought to the art therapy session in the same way. Free association to the material can still be explored.

This brings us to the other important part of the therapist's intervention when she suggested that Kim drew images of his family as a way of helping him begin to understand his complex, confused feelings. Gabrielle's method of working opens up the debate about focused and unfocused work. In the analytic model, the session is structured only by the time boundaries. The therapist does not intervene by making suggestions as to what it might be useful to work on. The material that evolves is seen to link with unconscious communications and to represent what is the most important to the client at the time. Gabrielle has chosen a more focused way of work. She actively influenced what happened in the relationship by suggesting it might be useful if Kim explored some images around his family. She did this in response to the surfacing of a lot of free-floating anxiety about his family. She believed that the act of focusing him at this stage would be containing for him, make his painfully chaotic world safe for him.

Gabrielle describes clearly her thinking behind this intervention as Kim was presenting an overwhelming sense of confusion and preoccupation with his family which he found difficult to articulate. If we raise the question of why the therapist asked Kim to draw his family, there may have been some underlying anxiety about being overwhelmed that was around between therapist and client – that, if Kim began to think and express his feelings about his family, this would overwhelm the therapist, a transference response to his experience of mother. Also it might be that the therapist's response was also one of being potentially overwhelmed – that this was of such importance to Kim and her response was to give herself some way of unconsciously protecting herself. If in the transference Kim had experienced the therapist as overwhelming, this would have led to him feeling persecuted and a possible reaction of withdrawal, which is what had happened with the first therapist. By suggesting that he focus the image, we can see how the image can act as an important container as the transference is channelled into it. This had the effect of working through feelings of being overwhelmed by enabling the images to hold them without having the same persecutory effect. They could therefore be contained for future work, if necessary, when Kim felt able to look at them. The sense of being mutually overwhelmed and overwhelming was therefore diffused from the immediate interpersonal space between therapist and client into the images which facilitated a space in which it could become conscious and worked through.

Another way of understanding this is in terms of the idea of the 'good-enough' mother. Winnicott (1965) describes this concept in terms of early mother–baby relationships and it forms the basis of adequate maternal care in meeting the needs of the infant. If this has been experienced, then this allows the baby the essential preparation for healthy development and growth in later life. This relationship is often reflected in the therapeutic alliance in terms of what the client is searching for and experiences in the transference and how this is experienced by the therapist. In Kim's situation, even though he describes clearly his difficulties with his mother in terms of carrying her emotional needs, it seems that he had a good-enough experience of mother in his early life and to some extent his relationship seemed a reparative one. He was trying to make up for this in some way and maybe this is also reflected in his relationship with the therapist. She needed to respond to his needs by being there and available to him and be a 'good-enough' therapist – perhaps to make up for his previous experience.

To return again to the image, what is interesting is its clarity, which forms a sharp contrast to the confusion of his emotional state. His description of the various members of his family and his feelings about his position among them are clearly illustrated and he is then able to articulate this to the therapist. The cues to his anxiety not to be invaded and fears of experiencing the therapist as persecutory are clearly stated through the image. Kim describes how he produced symbols for Gabrielle which he did not feel happy with, but there seems underlying this the fear of making a mess. His family seemed to stir up such messy feelings that creating a symbolic order was one way of giving control to his fear of making a mess and therefore exposing the 'mess' of his family.

Kim's description of the image and his understanding of the situation help the clarification of his feelings and of his role within the family. He comments on how he uses external things as a façade, like the television, and equally he describes his brother as a bulldozer, although he did not draw him like this. Here we see how, by bringing the family members into focus, some expression of feeling can be given to each. Kim is keen to put his own anger onto his brother, by giving him licence to smash things up like a bulldozer. He also describes how the bits have been 'cut off' and fall into bits at the bottom of the framework. This detail of the image was not picked up by the therapist and indeed it is hard to see it in the picture. This shows us a useful example of the process of internal work in making the image and, although some aspects are not named, it still has the effect of working through. It is too difficult to make sense of the Oedipal rage that is brought into focus here. The image shows it, but it is not conscious within the family. The image, however, holds this for the client and its significance remains for exploration at a later date.

It is possible, however, that this is what the therapist was picking up when she first noticed the sharp-edged spear. She came to understand this symbolised his mother, which is very different from the impotent portrayal of his father. Likewise, the difference between the images of his sister and two brothers again is important. It seems that he tended to define himself at this stage in terms of the others in the family and his experience of them– the denied femininity of his sister, the elusive, distant brothers that got away and the fury that this aroused, and the contrast between the penetrating, potent mother and the flaccid amorphous father. This portrayal raises the question of sexuality and models of potency and power within the family. Some of the confusion can be seen to be expressed in the overtly sexual nature of the shapes that are assigned to each member of his family.

One of the main difficulties Kim brings is his sense of an idealised family – how they ought to be and the particular role models that are expected – and the guilt he describes in revealing his own family experience. His anxiety about talking about his family was contained in the therapy and to some extent the image helped this process. His reference to being a 'martyr' sounded as though he was expecting or feared humiliation. This can be understood as an identification with the father by whom he felt often ridiculed.

This links with another noticeable aspect of this image, which is its ambiguity. Is the grid repressive and holding him in, an ensnaring experience from which he cannot escape, or is it structure for flight, something he can begin to think about in terms of shape and size and something he can work within and which in some way provides the beginnings of containment? He describes his sense of lack of parenting, and therefore his lack of experience of being understood and contained. However, the piercing, penetrating mother might be also supporting him. She gained his attention as he understood her experience, and he learnt to be an empty shell for her needs. In this sense he became a parent for her as he contained her needs.

Containment, as in Bion's theory (1962), is essential in early psychic development. The ambiguity of this image seems to suggest the lack of it but also the beginnings of a framework for it. Kim describes it as a framework, like imprisonment, but not for all members of the family. Is he trapped or held by the therapist? The transference process is clearly shown in the image. The aspect of hope and optimism was being held on to by the therapist while Kim continued to struggle with his painful feelings and descend further into despair. It is worth considering at this stage whether it was helpful for Kim to get so quickly into this material, which is one effect of directing the images made, and the response of the therapist. If material of depth is being produced very quickly, there is a need to feel contained to tolerate this. The fundamental experience of being heard and understood has to be of greatest significance for Kim at this stage. There is evidence of this in the relationship. The effect is the simultaneous expression of the split between hope and despair in the image and is also taken on by both client and therapist. Klein (1959) explains splitting as the tendency of the infantile ego to split impulses and objects, which is a primal activity of the ego, and this tendency to split results in part from the fact that the early ego largely lacks coherence. 'Persecutory anxiety reinforces the need to keep separate the loved object from the dangerous one and therefore to split love from hate. For the young infant's self-preservation depends on his trust in a good mother' (Klein 1959: 8). At the time it was difficult for the therapist to make sense of the intense and confused feelings conveyed. From her notes, she had a genuine concern for Kim as she was the focus for the very powerful feelings. She describes the need to contain her own anxiety and spent a lot of time thinking about the situation as she realised the extent to which Kim was depressed, in despair and possibly suicidal. However, to hold on to the hope was critical at this stage as the images provided the language for communication but also the catalyst without which he might have withdrawn further and this material not have surfaced. The language of imagery enabled articulation and thus a way through his own struggle. The images were speaking ahead of the words.

The extent of the despair the therapist was able to understand clarified this process, which underlies the importance of and need for supervision for all therapeutic work so that this can be processed and understood in such a way that thinking can take place. If we think about the image and the therapist's response, Bion's (1962) notion of the container and the contained and Winnicott's (1965) idea of the holding environment would seem to be useful. It is the holding environment by mother, or mother figure, for the baby and infant, which allows the infant to explore and take risks, make sense of his world and begin setting down the foundations of the self. It is the mother's tolerance for the baby's angry projections, which she holds for the child and then hands back in a digestible form, that allows the small child to mature emotionally. In the same way, Gabrielle maintains an atmosphere or culture in which Kim can begin to explore his inner feelings rather than bury them deeper. Patrick Casement, in *On Learning from the Patient* (1987), has developed Winnicott's idea of holding when he writes about the nursing triad. He asks who is supporting the nursing mother when she is nursing, who is containing the container. For the therapist to feel truly engaged, it is important that she feels held and supported, hence the necessity for supervision which is clearly illustrated here.

Consideration of these basic needs provides a useful model for therapy. The therapeutic approach by the therapist reminds us of the work of Ernest Wolff (1988) whose work arose out of narcissism and was developed from the earlier work of Kohut (1984). Wolff's self object needs have been expanded in his belief that for the individual to maintain its cohesion, its vigour and its balance the healthy self needs to be embedded in a milieu that is experienced as constantly supplying a self-sustaining self object ambience. Hence, Wolff's concepts of nurturing, idealising, alter ego, adversarial and efficacy needs would seem to be central in Gabrielle's approach to the material Kim is bringing to these sessions.

Figure 3 Depression.

Chapter 6

Relationship with mother

KIM'S ACCOUNT

My mother and I had got along really well when I was a kid and she indulged my eccentricities: perming my hair for me when I was at school, buying me a second-hand electric guitar on passing my 'O' levels with flying colours, and one thing in particular was, for my eighteenth birthday, insisting that she paid for me to have my first piece of clothing made by my idol's tailor. He told me that it had already been cut for him but because of his recent death he never finished it. So I had something of HIS . . . in a way.

In those days I often used to take my mother shopping (usually window shopping) or just 'out' when my father was not around (he was often working late and at weekends). I also took my mother to pop concerts while my father stayed at home – I don't think he liked the loud music. My father and mother did not go out very often together and I suppose I was trying to make up for that lack in my mother's life, my father was quite happy to stay at home.

I don't think my mother thought much of the change to my next image – maybe because nobody could ever match my old idol in her opinion, but probably also because I started spending ridiculous amounts of money on the upkeep of the same. Maybe she started to think that it was not right for a young man to spend so much time and money on his appearance though she never said anything . . . much.

The friction between us began when I started a relationship with my assistant at work. We often had a drink and/or a meal after work and I arrived home late. I guess that all families encounter the 'This place is not a hotel' or 'if you don't like it here . . .' problem at some point, but at the time I found it very difficult being on the wrong side of my mother. We quarrelled a lot. I decided to leave home, at very short notice (one day) and just before Christmas. My mother was extremely upset about this and I think it took her some time to forgive me. I cannot blame her.

For some time after I had moved out, my mother had left my room as I had left it. The fact that I had left quite a bit of my 'stuff' behind might have something to do with this. But this added to the impression that my room remained untouched like a kind of shrine. Neither of my brothers who had to share a room were allowed to move into it. Eventually the room was redecorated.

With the downfall of my fashion career, the failure of a business venture, not being able to secure a place in a college and the end of the lease on my flat, I convinced myself that I had no alternative but to move back to my parents' house. The truth was that I was becoming more deeply depressed and was finding it difficult coping with life. I was having enough trouble trying to sort myself out without having to worry about food and bills. My depression was crippling me and I hoped moving back home would give me a 'breather' so I could concentrate on getting my life sorted out. I asked my parents (my mother in particular) if I could move back home for a short while until I knew where I would need to locate myself next.

Initially my mother was not very receptive to the idea but she did let me move back in on a temporary basis under certain conditions. Even so I was glad to be back in because I did not feel I was strong enough to have remained independent. Despite the fact that the room that had been mine was not being used I was told I could not have that room back. I could sleep in the living room on a camp bed. I felt as if this was their way of humiliating me, of making an example of me to my brothers and sister. I believe it was not pleasant for my brothers and sister to witness how the mighty had fallen, or accept that I was in such a bad situation that I had to swallow my pride and accept these conditions. Shortly afterwards one of my brothers left home and I was able to share the bedroom with the brother who was still living at home. This was not so bad except I sometimes felt that I was invading his privacy and he might resent that. I mean he had been waiting long enough to have a room to himself only to have his older brother return home and cramp his space.

Through not having a room of my own I had nowhere to work in peace and quiet. My parents let me put up a trestle table in the living room for which I was grateful because it obviously made the room untidy, though I was not allowed to use 'messy' materials and this limited the media in which I could execute my work. The television was always on and consequently the best time for me to work on my portfolio was after eleven when everybody was in bed; usually I worked till about 2 o'clock in the morning. I didn't have to get up early for work every morning because I worked four days a week and sometimes a late shift. My days off I would want to spend working (on my portfolio) to help improve my chances for getting a college place later that year. My mother was usually at home, she didn't go out on her own, and when I was there she had someone to talk to. . . .

The year and a half between leaving home and coming back had seen no improvements in my parents' marriage. My mother had rarely been anywhere special at all during that time and now she was also preoccupied with time, the passing of it, the lack of happiness in her marriage and growing old. And I was back, the only listening ear in the immediate family. Of course, her parents were there for her but, because of their advancing years, my mother tried not to burden them too much with her problems. I couldn't just turn my back and say, 'Sorry mum, I have a lot to do and I really must get on with it.' I gave as much time as I could but still felt guilty because I knew it was not enough.

I listened and gave her my thoughts and opinions on her predicament and tried to be supportive but it was very difficult. I felt as if I was being torn apart inside between the demands I made upon myself through trying to cope with my own unhappiness and also now having to find words of hope and encouragement for my mother. I felt so wretched myself and yet I was having to absorb even more bad feelings through trying to help my mother, and when I tried to help I felt as if I was giving her hollow truths and false hope because I myself had nothing to give, no advice, no optimism, no light at the end of the tunnel, because I had none myself.

I assume for many people their parents would have been the first they would tell if they had a problem, were unhappy, sad or depressed. I never told mine even when I had suicidal thoughts and there were several reasons why I kept my depression to myself.

My mother had plenty of her own problems and I couldn't burden her with mine even though I was prepared to accept the reverse. This may have to do with the fact that I did not want to be indebted any more to my parents than I was already for the roof over my head. I would accept the material support but could not possibly accept emotional support because it would have disadvantaged me too much . . . also I could not let them know how much of a mess I was in. I had already lost too much pride by asking to return home for a while. I did not think of talking to my father about my problems . . . we never talked much, but between them both I would have been too ashamed and embarrassed to talk about how sad I felt and that I could not see any point of carrying on any more. I knew I would have started crying if I did (which was why I needed someone whom I did not know to talk to, my pride would not be damaged . . . so much) and then what sort of position would I have been in with my parents? A very weak one indeed.

Having to fall in with the house routine of mealtimes and the television nearly always on just added to my frustration and increased my sense of hopelessness about being able to improve my work enough or to get enough done to secure a place at college in the following months. My situation was hopeless and I was trapped. I had no time to move out to lodgings, I was falling behind with the tasks I set myself and college interviews were looming. On occasions I worked all through the night to have an extra piece of work to take with me to the interviews. Not that it did me any good because I was then too tired to conduct myself in a positive manner – which would have been difficult anyway! Maybe I was making myself too tired so that I could have an excuse for not getting accepted at a college. I wanted to fail so I could have something else to be unhappy about and say, oh dear, nothing ever goes right for me. The possibility of anything going right for me didn't exist because I had been unhappy for so long that I had forgotten what it was like to have something to be pleased about.

The series of small sketches I did around this time were an attempt to try and convey the stress I felt, how close I was to breaking point. They are abstract representations of forces being applied to shapes being bent or cracking under the pressure, the pressure of carrying on with my life. Other visual metaphors I thought of were shattering glass or material being rent, tweezed apart and unravelled by the opposing forces of which I was caught in the middle. The fabric of my being was being worn thin and my soul was showing. I even drew myself as a small figure helpless in the shadow of a gigantic spider towering threateningly above me – I am not afraid of spiders myself but I used one because I know that many people do not like them.

I was not very pleased with these little pictures, not because of the scale, but because they just did not convey the difficulty and the effort I required to keep going in these adverse conditions and how I literally felt as if I was being torn apart. Every day was such a struggle and it was wearing me down – I really did not know how much longer I would be able to carry on if my situation did not change. These pictures were just visual metaphors, abstract representations with no emotion. In frustration and desperation I took some charcoal and tried to thrash it out on paper.

These messy pictures were more expressive and I found a little satisfaction in that. They were a different sort of picture, a type of image that was not mine, they were new and I was getting somewhere. Expression in art had always eluded me at school and, though my graphic approach got me good marks, I was aware that my work lacked something. I was finding a way of getting emotion into pictures as well as just meaning but, as with everything else in my life at the time, I couldn't really appreciate it.

Not a single thing in my life remained untainted by my depressions as I could not find joy in anything. I no longer listened to the music of my idols which had been so important to me as a 'boost to my batteries'. Even when I achieved something in my pictures for therapy or work for my portfolio my self-esteem was so low that it was impossible for me to even consider that I might have done something of some worth. This is how depression wears people down until they can no longer bear feeling sad all of the time.

I felt fairly ambivalent about taking these pictures along to Gabrielle.

Figure 4 Bending under the strain.

They were interesting images graphically but they simply did not convey the terrible burden of my situation and the struggle of keeping my sadness from overwhelming me. It was difficult for me to accept the strength that Gabrielle said was evident in my drawings. The shapes were bent, twisted and torn but they still remained whole, and there was colour in the pictures too. These were the clues to the inner strength I had! I told Gabrielle that they were just drawings and I really didn't have the strength that was in them, I felt as if I was running out of energy with which to carry on. But I said I would remember what she had told me and would think about it.

THERAPIST'S ACCOUNT

Kim was very depressed. He described an isolated, hermit-like existence, a fear of people and persecuted feelings towards himself. He continued to display a tense, rigid façade. His presentation was still immaculate, but felt unscathed and untouchable. In spite of this, I carried a belief that we would eventually make contact as I felt a glimmer of Kim's human face beneath the layers of façade. I felt a warmth towards him. Although Kim was not ready to show it, it was possible to see beneath the cold exterior.

It became clear to me, as Kim talked about his relationship with his family, that he was entangled in a very powerful relationship with his mother. As he spoke about her, there was a noticeable intensity about his feelings and a sense of being overwhelmed. He would become more anxious. In Kim's case this was demonstrated by an increased flatness in his mood and talking at a great speed without showing any affect. I decided to encourage Kim to do a series of pictures around his relationship with his mother. I suggested this as Kim seemed to be involved in a paralysing dyadic relationship with his mother and my sense was that this would need further exploration.

It seemed to me at this stage that Kim's sense of depression was rooted in a need to develop a separate sense of who he was and disentangle from his merged sense of mother. From what he said about his mother, it seemed that he felt the receptacle for much of her emotional needs; he would have to tolerate hearing about all the unhappy detail of his parents' marriage. He carried the burden of her frustration and lack of her own personal development. He had become the support for her emotional difficulties and he was parenting his mother, which had become the pattern of their relationship over many years.

While recognising the overwhelming and burdening feelings Kim felt in relationship to his mother, we also need to put the relationship in a context and acknowledge her experience. We can speculate that it is more than likely that she did not have the capacity to find space for her own children because this was probably never done for her. Many of her needs may have not been met or were not responded to. As a young mother, she had to struggle with the experience of a physically and emotionally absent husband. Moreover, we live in a society which places unrealistic pressures on mothers without sufficient support and therefore we need to recognise the emotional, social and cultural pressures that made her task so difficult. While I hold this in mind in my attempt to understand Kim's experience, it is not my concern at this point. My task is to understand his world and hopefully in time, when he feels he can understand and integrate his experience, then he might be able to put his relationship with mother into a wider context.

Kim talked about his mother burdening him with her worries. He described how she, in the past, had gone into detail about the breakdown of the relationship with her husband. She would talk about her disappointment, her frustration and would turn to him emotionally for the support that she was not getting from her husband. Kim described how he was a good listener and it became his role to act as the peacemaker or pacifier in the family. This gave little room for the expression of his anxieties, doubts and worries. It would seem that over the years he had learnt to suppress this part of himself. He talked about how she would never enquire about how he was emotionally or have any understanding of what he was doing.

Kim brought to the session his anger and frustration about the experience he had with his mother on the telephone that week. She had phoned him because the family hamster had died. She was feeling particularly devastated by this. Kim was the listener and the digester of her experience. She did not ask how he was or what was happening. He at the time had been feeling isolated, depressed and hopeless about himself. Kim was able to talk about how this echoed the communication between them. It was as if he had always had to parent her, attend to her emotional life, but she had been unable to do the same for him. Kim had little memory of the interaction that took place as a small child. It is however possible to speculate that this pattern was part of his early experience. His mother was so consumed with her own disappointments that she had difficulty attending to her own children's needs as separate and allowing them their own experience that was not merely an extension of her own. His images reflected his sense of being weighed down, burdened, intruded upon by his mother. In the therapy, there was an opportunity to separate a definite and boundaried sense of who he was.

At the time he was consumed by this relationship it was necessary to hold in mind the family constellation. Kim was not the only member of the family that was not functioning. His sister was being treated for an eating disorder. His brothers had found a way of distancing themselves from the family. His father's role was to remain passive and he seemed unable to offer protection or distance from the conflict between him and his wife. His withdrawal would seem to have engulfed the children deeper into the family conflict.

Kim did a series of drawings in his exploration of his depression and relationship with his mother. He made several small, well-executed, contained and powerful images to express their symbolic interaction. The pencil marks were executed with honesty and the charcoal with speed and strength, perhaps facilitating the expression of true emotion. There was a sensitivity and authenticity to these images which was beginning to show another aspect of himself, unknown and buried to Kim at the time. After completing the images, he felt depleted and overwhelmed by feelings of worthlessness. He talked of feeling more despair and an increase in his suicidal thoughts. He discussed at length whether he should start taking anti-depressants again and asked for my opinion. He profoundly communicated his level of despair at this point, and I was aware that, in order to be able to offer containment for him, it was necessary to show my concern and not my anxiety. I acknowledged and addressed his deep fears and suicidal thoughts, but also communicated my belief that his work was very powerful and painful and involved the expression of the feelings he was experiencing. Because of the communication in his pictures, I had a belief that he had the capacity to tolerate and go beyond this despair, and an authentic creativity was emerging. In the first picture (Figure 3,

'Depression'), Kim made a series of powerful swirling charcoal marks. There is a fluidity to them. He saw them as ensnaring and felt trapped by them. He saw this as symbolising his depression, enveloping and overwhelming him. Behind the heavy charcoal lines is a fainter yellow image which he saw as himself. He saw it as faint and subsumed by the mass of charcoal swirls. Although faint, I felt it could be seen but at the time it was unavailable to Kim. In the second picture (Figure 4, 'Bending under the strain') there is a heavy boulder sculptured shape weighing heavily on another sculptured boulder. On first impression, it is as if the second stone is overwhelmed by the pressing weight of the heavier sculpture and will collapse or snap. On reframing the image or looking again, it looks as if the smaller of the two images has a spring-like quality and has the ability to spring or push away. The smaller sculptured shape on the right has a suggestion of colour and perhaps of life separate from the other. The foundations on which the boulders are placed look sturdy enough to tolerate the separation.

Two weeks later Kim drew the same foundation under a heavier weight. The foundations had cracked open but there seemed to be a little more solidity to them. Perhaps this was in some way what Kim was experiencing in the therapeutic relationship. It was as if his foundations/his internal self was cracking open but, in his relationship with me, he had the possibility of firmer foundation. This was to coincide with his intensified feelings of moving into a deeper depression and an overwhelming sense of bleakness.

The next image he was to draw (Figure 5, 'Caught in the shadow') is a huge spider with a dense black shadow. Kim was to call this image 'under the shadow'. He saw the spider squashing the shadow below and the shadow was him. He said that, after he made this picture, he felt exhausted and empty. He talked of getting nowhere and everything was pointless. He could see no way out. In spite of his feeling so overwhelmed and swamped, the picture did not convey only despair to me. Next to the shadow was another shadow, perhaps his, that conveyed another part of Kim that as yet was unknown to him.

His mood, behaviour and words communicated despair and hopelessness at this point. As an art therapist I had another level of communication from Kim that was being clearly expressed in the images. This was not conscious to Kim, but made explicit to me by the image. The glimmer of colour and the possible resilience in the images that symbolised Kim communicated themselves to me, if not to him. It allowed me to carry the hope and belief in the possibility of his development beyond his known depression. Although the pictures on the surface were bleak, the sensitivity and honesty with which they expressed aspects of Kim suggested the possibility of Kim being able to find out who he was, as a separate and real person. Kim was beginning to express some of the emotional pain and confusion onto paper. Although this made the images for what they really

Figure 5 Caught in the shadow.

were – frightening, dark and haunting – at first it was to allow him to feel no longer overwhelmed by the internal confusion of thoughts and feelings. By finding a way to unjumble his internal world, he was to begin the process of separating out thoughts and feelings that was, in time, to improve his mastery of himself and his environment. His internal world was to be no longer a mass of uncontained and all invading thought. It would allow sufficient psychic space for him to develop parts of himself. It was the beginning of setting himself the foundation of being able to separate out the process of thinking and feeling.

OVERVIEW

Here we see the continuation of the central dynamic of feeling overwhelmed – Kim's sense of his mother becomes the focus for these feelings which is picked up by the therapist. She responds by inviting Kim to express his feelings through some images around his relationship with his mother. In the session, there is the question of who is feeling overwhelmed by whom: in the transference Kim might be in touch with this by feeling overwhelmed by the therapist and also in his fear that his needs might overwhelm her. The therapist clarified this by noting this in the transference and how it was becoming clear within their relationship. It is possible that this was not yet fully conscious, as Kim's sense of being merged with mother might have communicated itself in terms of his need to merge with the therapist – hence the sense of being overwhelmed. Here we can also see some indications of early infantile relationship between mother and baby that are emerging. As the transference becomes clearer, the therapist suggests he explore his relationship with mother. This has the effect of creating a safe space in which Kim can do this by allowing the therapist to carry the hope and the belief in him – as any mother would with a tiny, newborn baby. By describing his experience of mother as someone unable to acknowledge his needs and anticipate and respond to his infantile desires, this has painted for the therapist the image of a 'bad' mother and by this he is communicating his needs to the therapist. This leads to the idealisation of the therapist as Kim searches for an experience of the 'good' mother. What is interesting is that we have seen how the therapist, in already responding to many of his needs and understanding his anxieties in terms of feeling the need for privacy and space, time and structure, has set up a framework in which this idealised state can develop. Kim has been able to express his enormous dependency needs and his communication is heard by the therapist, which is particularly important as he feels no possibility of emotional support from his family.

The therapist or the mother becomes a selfless screen onto which the baby/client can project his love and hate, his fears and frustrations and acts as a container for the baby's emotional needs while not overwhelming the child with her own unmet needs. In Gabrielle, Kim could begin to experience this. In the counter-transference, Gabrielle describes how she must meet his uncontained needs by showing concern but not anxiety – she is withholding her own feelings so that he is not denied his. This is important, as it might be that the therapist was in touch with something significant in Kim's early life – that his mother did not encourage Kim's expression of his own needs as she might have been overwhelmed by them. It is possible that the same dynamic is operating unconsciously in the therapist's response by suggesting to Kim that he draws images of this relationship rather than allow the full force of its exploration to be experienced between client and therapist. The transference feelings can be channelled into the images and Kim clearly describes the sense of feeling torn apart, trapped, and that the images convey the idea of pressure, tensions and being near to breaking point. Making the images has the effect of clarifying, intensifying and bringing to the surface these feelings, which are then worked through. The images are thus important as a means of focusing these feelings, which of course is not an option available to an overwhelmed mother in responding to her infant's needs.

There is also the question of whether this served to reinforce the idealisation – the real mother remained all 'bad' – which enabled the therapist to be all 'good' in the transference. The depth of Kim's sense of deprivation of mother in terms of meeting his needs is directly proportional to the resulting degree of idealisation of the therapist. The split is thus maintained, but it was helpful for Kim to be able to explore his feelings by using the distance of the idealisation as it begins the process of articulation through his images, which are fascinating in their portrayal of his experience. In the previous 'family picture' there was ambiguity about feelings of being trapped or torn apart in the framework of the image; the meaning has now become clearer for Kim and he is able to articulate this for himself as the process develops over time. Once again we see how visual literacy can emerge out of pain, confusion and sense of overwhelming depression, but this can lead to unfolding of yet further, deeper despair.

This reminds us of Bion's (1967) ideas of the relationship between the emerging sense of self of the growing infant and the mother's capacity to consolidate meaning. In the therapeutic relationship, Kim is asking for consolidation and reaffirmation of his feelings – in a sense to have his experience validated. Gabrielle has reinforced Kim's use of images and this confirming experience has a positive effect. He can place his immaculate self into the execution of his images on which the therapist comments several times. This has the effect of releasing the underlying suppressed feelings of hopelessness and helplessness that are brought to the surface – just like a baby.

Kris (1975) identified aspects of creativity in terms of the artist's ability to tap unconscious sources without losing control by 'regression in the service of the ego'. The artist/client can be seen as someone who 'lets go' by allowing aspects of inner self to take over through the continual interplay between creation and criticism which leads to relaxation and regression. It is because of this collapse of ego control that it is essential for the therapist to have empathy with the creative process and we can see how this process is occurring here. Kim is becoming in touch with some early infantile needs, most crucially dependence on mother. In parallel with this is the emergence of his creativity in which his real self, previously repressed, can emerge into the vacuum. This demonstrates one important function of creativity in that he can find his own way separate from mother by objectifying her in this way. The therapist comments on the symbolic relationship with mother as expressed in the first image (Figure 3), but this suggests that this relationship might be seen as almost symbiotic – fused and merged together in their difficulties. It is as if they are locked together and are mutually overwhelmed in this relationship and there is a sense of unravelling and tearing apart.

In the second image (Figure 4), the image seems more grounded and solid. There is a suggestion that each figure is reliant on the other to hold each other up and Kim portrays the tension as if it might snap. As Kim describes, his feelings towards his father are now coming more into focus and there is a confusion in his mind about his 'role' in the family. He describes how he cannot talk to his father but takes on an ambiguous role for his mother. He feels that taking her out and acting almost as her partner and companion in his father's absence brought them close together. However, when he chose another partner and established a relationship on his own, the closeness with his mother changed to a relationship of friction and exclusion. When he expressed his own sexuality in the development of independent relationships, he sensed there was no space for him in mother's mind as a man, only as a child. By remaining withdrawn and distanced from the family, father did not protect Kim from his mother's demands and, while Kim enjoyed her attention and indulged in the idea of them as a 'couple' for some time, when this changed he was left angry and excluded and alone.

His feelings of confusion and ambivalence towards his father were compounded by this situation and left Kim struggling with his rather muddled fantasies about both mother and father. He seems to associate his own feelings of weakness and powerlessness with his father. Father's emotional absence made the relationship complex in terms of the resolution of the Oedipal conflicts generated between mother and son. Klein provides us with a useful explanation here.

> However good are the child's feelings towards both parents, aggressiveness and hate also remain operative. One expression of this is the rivalry with the father which results from the boy's desires towards the mother and all the phantasies linked with them. Such rivalry finds expression in the Oedipus complex, which can be clearly observed in children of three, four or five years of age. This complex exists, however, very much earlier and is rooted in the baby's first suspicions of the father taking the mother's love and attention away from him.
>
> (Klein 1959)

She continues

> The Oedipus complex is thus not a matter only of feelings of hate and rivalry towards one parent and love towards the other, but feelings of hate and a sense of guilt also enter in connection with the rival parent. Many conflicting emotions therefore centre upon the Oedipus complex.
>
> (Klein 1959: 7)

Kim's confused feelings were clearly expressed in the series of drawings, but there was also a process of clarification from the previous image in which his family were conveyed as more amorphous shapes. The solid forms are touching and are in contact and as such are making a space between them. This space could be understood to be a container for his feelings as Kim struggles to make sense of his relationships. This marks a shift from the first entangled charcoal image and seems to connect with the unresolved relationship with father which is now brought more sharply into focus in the exploration of the images. Within the Oedipal situation, mother/therapist have at times been interchangeable in the transference, and there are signs of the emergence of some fantasies around the therapist. However, what is also noticeable about the figure shapes is that they are decapitated, they have no heads, which does not allow any thinking about these fantasies and desires. The image clearly shows the dilemma and is poised with ambivalence. If one figure moves, the other will be squashed or collapse and so they have to be held together by this tension. The tension conveys ideas of springing back or might express his feelings of mother leaning on him – or is he leaning on her, and or the therapist? Basically it feels too dangerous for anyone to move.

In the third image (Figure 5) there is a sense of incorporation or conquest or resolution from the first two images. This image invites many kinds of associations around the idea of being devoured or devouring, eating up and disappearing back into mother's stomach, a return to the womb. It is a sinister image and Kim describes himself as the helpless figure overshadowed by the enormous spider. It is the spider that symbolically holds the meaning in the picture. Many species of spider eat the male after copulation and the image seems to suggest fantasies connected to this, possibly an expression of mother's unconscious wishes and also his own terms of wanting to be back inside mother and merging symbiotically with her.

In the transference with the therapist he is working through these very difficult feelings. Kim speaks of doing 'messy' pictures which were more expressive of these messy feelings. He is in touch with some primitive, painful material which is impossible to articulate at this stage. Although his depression is deepening, it is important to allow this regression and for this resolution to take place. The containment by the therapist and the images enables this process to occur at a deeper level than in the previous sessions and we can see clearly how this process is developing. The images are conveying aspects of his experience to the therapist, which she can see but he is not yet able to, and this offers us a clear account of this process. The images for him convey his worst fears and most unacceptable, despised fantasies and aspects of himself which are surfacing into consciousness and are central to his preoccupations and suicidal thoughts.

Figure 6 Harlequin.

Chapter 7

In the cocoon

KIM'S ACCOUNT

Gabrielle suggested I tried making a picture with colour and I drew the harlequin in an effort to show how colourful a character I used to be and wished that I could go back to being. Maybe I was fantasising in a *Marvel Comic Book* fashion about myself, trying to endow myself with powers that I never actually had. But I HAD been a colourful person once, not just in a clothes sense but also in nature and humour. I had suppressed my sense of humour over the years of wanting to be my idols. They were very serious (as far as I knew), and never joked or laughed about, so neither did I. This was a shame because I used to be funny and able to make people laugh. All I seemed to do these days was to drag them down and never having any good news for my friends was another reason I cut myself off from them.

So I drew a colourful figure to represent me in the past and how I would like to be again and, while drawing it, I rediscovered something I had lost, forgotten about, the simple pleasure or joy in making a picture. I revelled in the freedom, just making patterns and filling them in as I wished, without having to worry if they were wrong or right in any sense, because there was no pressure, no importance attached to them, unlike my portfolio preparation upon which I believed my future depended. This exercise brought back memories of primary school and how much I looked forward to and enjoyed the art lessons, and the memories made me smile to myself as I drew.

But there was something else too, something that went beyond the act of drawing. Maybe I was fantasising but as I worked I started feeling excited, the thought occurred to me that, as I was making this picture, there might be a parallel in a magical sort of way and I was actually putting colour back into myself. This gave me some enthusiasm to make it powerful, hence the light radiating from the centre of the being, and I was very happy with the way it was looking until I came to the head. The head caused me a problem. I did not know how to fill it in, with a pattern, with a face or both. I did not know what to do and became disappointed because I could not finish it. Part of the reason for my disappointment was that, being unfinished, it could not be effective in the magical way I had imagined. Another was that it could not be a candidate for the wall.

The pictures on the walls of the therapy room had been some motivation for me. I wanted to have one of mine up there with them in this tiny little gallery. Why? Because I did not want to be another nameless client, the few pictures on the walls were good and did not all show suffering. Most of them were positive but there was one that struck me as melancholy and made quite an impression upon me. I wanted to be recognised along with these others, and it was a matter of ego as well that I should be able to make a picture good enough to be displayed; after all I was good at art once, and surely I could match their standard.

But if I was more depressed than they (as I believed no one felt as unhappy as I) then I should be able to make a picture that was better than theirs, that would stand out and say that a very unhappy young man had been here. A tiny little bit of fame in a way, it seemed as if that was all I could ever hope to achieve in respect of that four-letter word.

Even though I had not been able to finish it (and it was not good enough for the wall) it had been a positive exercise and I was comfortable about showing it to Gabrielle. I was prepared for a criticism of its childish naivety and use of coloured pencils (not a real artist's material, I considered) and expressed my disappointment at being unable to finish the drawing. Gabrielle commented on the positive aspects, the colourful patterns and how they radiated from the being and insisted that I have some colour in ME because, if I had not, I would not have been able to imagine this Harlequin. This made sense and I had to accept it, though I felt a long way removed from this gaudy being. Gabrielle suggested that, as a reminder to myself, I should put this picture somewhere that I would see it often. Because of my situation at home I decided to keep it in my briefcase so I would see the Harlequin whenever I opened it. Once again that feeling of magic arose as I started to feel that the picture was in fact endowed with a power and it became a kind of talisman to me.

With regard to the head, or lack of it, Gabrielle simply told me not to worry about the face because maybe I would know how to fill it in at a later date, and this gave me a little hope that it was possible for me to get better, and back to the way I used to be.

Four years later I can now see my face in it . . . sometimes.

THERAPIST'S ACCOUNT

Kim had just been through the intense experience of making a series of drawings about his family. The images he had made of him and the struggle with his feelings of hopelessness had left him feeling depleted and drained. This I thought at the time was partly as a result of their intensity and genuineness and the painful material they were evoking for him. However, behind the black charcoal and pencil marks, there had been a glimmer of

Figure 1 Early image.

Figure 2 Trap.

Figure 3 Depression.

Figure 4 Bending under the strain.

Figure 5 Caught in the shadow.

Figure 6 Harlequin.

Figure 7 Breaking out.

Figure 8 Against the tide.

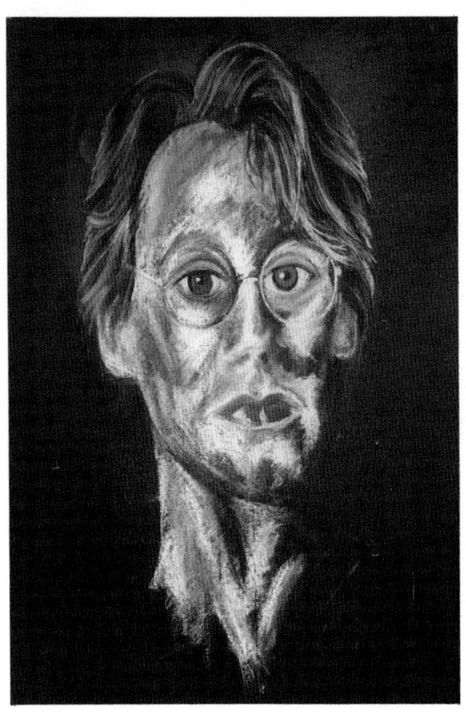

Figure 9 Self-portrait.

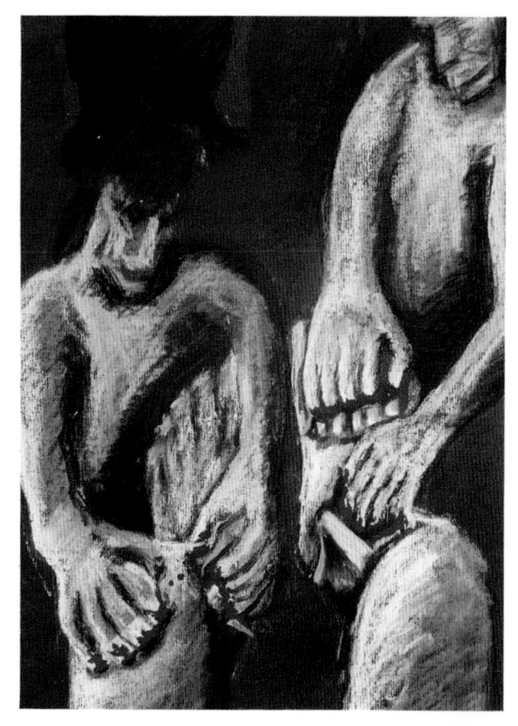

Figure 10 Under the skin.

Figure 11 Barrier.

Figure 12 Gabrielle.

Figure 13 Leaving the maze.

colour. At this time, Kim could not see the colour. He could see the cracking foundations, the swirling marks, but the colour eluded him. In response to this colour, I had suggested that he tried to make a picture using colour. I felt my task was to help him truly experience what was in the picture. At the time the colour was buried, unknown and unavailable to him. The picture spoke a language that communicated a part of Kim that I was able to see, but hidden and split off from Kim. I was trying to help translate an artistic symbol into an understood communication.

When introducing the idea of exploring the use of colour and sharing another part of himself with me, I hoped that he would find this buried part of himself which he could begin to recreate. It would not be a false creation, a false persona, but a development of a genuine hidden part of his personality.

'Harlequin' (Figure 6) was the picture Kim was to produce. It was a tightly cocooned figure, the arms held very tightly by its side. The head was only a faint pencil mark. There was a beautiful burst of colour from the centre of the figure. The rest of the figure was coloured in a gentle graduation of colour. The first image that came into my head was of a mummy figure that had been embalmed. Kim was able to share some of the pleasure he had experienced in the making of the picture. He described how he had enjoyed becoming involved in the act of colouring. He described how it seemed to have acted as a gentle therapeutic exercise which put him in touch with some early childhood memories. The act of colouring had allowed him to enter into a playful activity that had been unavailable to Kim for a long time. It had been able to lift him temporarily out of his overwhelming need to control for fear of fragmentation. While this might have been a transient experience, it opened up the possibility of repetition of such an experience. The cocoon was a way of protecting himself and building up some defences, it was also simultaneously opening up the possibilities of rekindling a part of him. The colouring is gentle, not wild and expressive. It has a soothing containing quality.

This picture was not to be a catalyst for 'peeling off' more of his protective layers, but was to represent symbolically the covering up of himself. In context, this was perhaps appropriate, as I felt he was frightened of laying himself more open, he was depressed and was experiencing more suicidal thoughts. It was as if he knew that it was necessary to replace some of his protection in the mummified figure, but he was also to allow in a chink of light by his experimentation with colour.

This was the first time in the sessions that he had been able to communicate feelings not only of despair, but of possible hope. His ability to mix colour, to blend and shade, was perhaps symbolically representing some development in his ability to tolerate ambiguity and uncertainty. While this was communicated in the image, Kim was not able to articulate this to me. The image was speaking before him, as this part of himself had not been integrated but was an indicator of what was possible.

The cocoon or mummy-like figure was a contained, tightly bound shape.

It suggested to me some form of self-containment or self-binding. Kim, although despairing, was able to demonstrate the capacity for a degree of self-containment and had perhaps begun to internalise some holding of the therapeutic relationship. The picture of the cocoon seemed to me to have simultaneously represented both a break-through and a risk in terms of his use of colour and a putting on of layers, as in the act of covering up. As he was letting in one burst of sunlight, he was also putting back in place some protective layers. Just as the chrysalis weaves some layers to protect himself in preparation for his metamorphosis, it would seem that Kim's image was a symbolic voicing of this metaphor. The cocoon builds up his defence structure in preparation for breaking out and breaking through.

At the time of making the image, Kim was able to communicate a glimmer of hope. Previously I had experienced his isolation, the monotony, the fears and the despair and had communicated his worthless and meaningless experience when contemplating suicide. The cocoon harlequin figure was to become a symbol for Kim and he shared how he thought it was imbued with some 'magical mystery qualities'. This felt to me as though Kim was beginning to recognise some of his own potential power, his ability to influence both himself and others. He said he was troubled by the incompleteness of the image. I was able to communicate that perhaps it was important that the image was incomplete and he might feel able to return to it later and retain the experience of his ambivalence. Perhaps it represented the remaking of his emotional interior and this would involve the uncertainty of not knowing.

Kim described how he felt dull, boring and as if there was nothing inside. He could not believe that anyone would want to spend time with him. He had withdrawn from his friends because he thought he was boring and had nothing to offer them. I sensed he feared he might bore me and that I might get fed up with him. Was I the mummy figure embalmed? Perhaps one of the reasons Kim worked so hard to create such powerful images was his own fear that I would lose interest in him. My concern was to communicate to him that I was not accepting him for his pictures but for himself. He needed to know that I was not going to lose interest in him.

In Kim's earlier family drawings, behind the intense charcoal marks and the gentle pencil, there had been a glimmer of colour. We had talked about this glimpse of colour and what this might mean for him. He was able to dimly recall some more colourful aspects of his personality which he had spent the last few years trying to suppress. This led to Kim sharing with me how, before his overwhelming depression, he had spent a great deal of time and energy developing a flamboyant and exotic external persona. When this collapsed he was left feeling completely colourless. He experienced himself as arid and grey. The colour had all been on the outside and he had been unable to internalise it as a real part of his experience.

Working with this communication I had raised the issue of colour, and suggestions such as these had now become part of the pattern of our relationship. But this needed to be thought about in terms of the balance of power between us, and also his need to be compliant for fear of rejection by me. The act of compliance mirrored his earlier relationship with mother so graphically described. Was he fearful that, if he did not seem to be going along with my 'scheme', I might not see him as worthy of treatment? Had he in earlier significant relationships internalised a model of compliance as a means of avoiding conflict? Had he in our relationship become caught in an idealised transference whereby he had totally handed over all the power to me as 'all knowing' and 'all curing'. These questions had to be held in mind and worked with as the material presented itself.

OVERVIEW

The process of this session and the image itself presents us with an interesting paradox. The image, a body shape with no head, suggests protection, framework for survival, layers of defence and yet also colour, radiation, brightness and change. The change can be seen in the striking difference from the previous images in terms of its colour, attention to detail and complexity. The outer framework and grids have moved to an inside structure – aspects of inside and outside experience are moving together. Perhaps this represents elements of incorporation that were evident in the previous session. This process, which could be seen as consolidation or internalisation, is described by Kim as he feels the colour is going inside him. At the same time, he described an inner freedom of creative expression.

By making the image, Kim has a means of allowing inner feelings and deep preoccupations to surface and become conscious, but at the same time making available to him the possibility of protecting himself, remaining in control and preventing his ultimate fear of disintegration or annihilation. He is struggling with the dilemma of how much of himself to risk, how much to expose and some degree of understanding emerges throughout the session.

In their interactions, the therapist had noted the glimpse of colour in the previous image and this suggests some communication through the image that light and hope can emerge. By making this conscious, Kim is now prepared to try out and risk some experimentation with colour and yet is able to hold on to his own way of remaining in some degree of control and not over-exposing himself. He describes how this makes him feel excited and evokes memories of primary school, his teacher and his childlike feelings at the time. He expresses a sense of freedom from being judged on his drawings which directly affects the feelings towards both the image and the therapist. Both are the container for the intense feelings in the transference relationship.

This seems to be the central dynamic developing in terms of the relationship between therapist and client – can the therapist be seen as different from his intrusive experience of mother and how much can Kim risk exposing his true feelings? – that is, can he trust her to understand and contain the depth of his emotions, including possibly unacceptable thoughts and fantasies he might have had about his teacher and the therapist? The two figures are intertwined in his mind, the feelings resurface when he fears a critical response from Gabrielle when showing her this image. The image contains both acceptable and also unacceptable parts of himself – in Kim's mind it is not 'good enough' to go on the wall, it is incomplete and does not have a face – symbolically this may indicate a difficulty in facing up to these very difficult, genuine and excitable feelings that are beginning to surface. No head perhaps does not allow the capacity for thinking – to be faceless implies anonymity.

The links between this session and the previous one are important. The theme of mother shifts to an 'embalmed mummy' which was the first association that the therapist made to the image. Mother is still the central figure in both transference and counter-transference but she is 'preserved' in Kim's mind which allows him the freedom for other fantasies to emerge.

The therapist is responding to the strong dynamic of dependency and we note how this is important in terms of Winnicott's view of the emergence of the real self. She is in touch with Kim's real fear of disintegration if he were to expose his true feelings and the power of the art medium has so far accelerated this process. The art-making process can often be a powerful catalyst for the expression of unconscious material and therefore it is important to recognise this. The therapist is in touch with a need to hold back, to consolidate these shifts so far and act as a solid container for these feelings. Gabrielle responds in this way as she is confident of the communication through the image and allows the potential of the creative process to enable change in this way. The process remains in the image but is recognised and worked with by the therapist. She picks up the sense of feeling 'all knowing' and 'all curing' but, while holding on to the hope in the midst of the despair, she can also invest in him her belief that self-expression is a way out of his despair and the colour is an indication of this. She has been able to see what he cannot and, by her helping him to notice this, he can introject this and take it in for himself.

There also may be a sense that this is her way of giving back to Kim some of the colour that he initially invested in the therapist – her clothes and appearance were most important in the early sessions and he has produced another sort of 'clothing', swaddling or protective skin. There is an aura of both life and death portrayed by the mummy-like embalmed figure, but the 'life' is generated by the therapist's ability to think of colour in this way while Kim is struggling with his despair. Is this colourful but closed-in person how he wants to portray himself? He feels relieved that the therapist has connected with his use of colour, but he struggles with the idea of being a 'colourful' character on the outside. He says he wants to distance himself from this 'gaudy being' and is hiding behind the colour, feeling empty and drab inside, which is his experience at the moment. The external 'cloak' of colour might again serve to emphasise his false self which he is presently trying to shed and discard. He identified with the therapist early on in terms of her clothes but we can here see a shift in his ability to see that this is not his real self – his real self is struggling to emerge in a different form.

The importance of the colour becomes clear as Kim describes the magical element of this in the image through which he can feel empowered. The image takes on a magical quality. Making the picture makes him feel excited but also scared. Schaverien (1992) helps us to understand the significance of this process. She suggests that the result of engagement by the artist in image making is that the image becomes 'embodied' as a form of transference which takes place in relation to the picture. The embodied image is an object of transference. Earlier in the process of therapy it was noted that the images were 'diagrammatic' but in the previous session Kim describes the moment of change in himself when he invests his emotions in his drawings. As Kim describes, the picture comes to be experienced as magically invested and so capable of 'working wonders'; unconsciously the picture may come to be identified with parts of himself. Through Kim's relation to the embodied image, the Harlequin as he calls it, differentiation begins to take place and eventually he is separate enough from the image to speak about the experience of it and the picture object mediates the experience of different levels of consciousness.

> The picture which embodies a transference may come to be additionally empowered as a talisman or a token within the therapeutic relationship. This valuing of the object is a consequence of the pictorial elements, but its effects extend beyond the picture to the relationship between the people. An object which is empowered within the therapeutic context will have impact on both the transference and counter-transference.
>
> (Schaverien 1992: 137)

Schaverien explains that the therapeutic relationship is animated by the picture which reveals elements which otherwise may remain invisible. Unconsciously the client may paint the therapist into the fabric of the picture, thus revealing the configuration of the transference. The picture which is a reflection of the transference may evoke a conscious counter-transference response from both client and therapist. Therefore the picture is incorporated and integrated into the therapeutic relationship and is valued in a way which relates to the affect it embodies. In this way the image may become a talisman and is affectively empowered.

We can see this process clearly in Kim's account of making this image. The embodied image is not a mental image but the process of making a preconceived image is relinquished. There is no immediate explanation in words and it transcends what is consciously known. We can see how, in the making, the picture developed in unexpected ways and took a form which was not predicted and surprised its maker. The intensity of a preconscious image is articulated into a pictorial form. In doing so, the colours, shapes and figurations reveal previously unconscious aspects of Kim's internal world. The picture was the object which mobilised the affect, brought it into the present to be intensely experienced in relation to the image.

The mechanism of projective identification may be part of the internal process operating when the picture becomes empowered in such a way. As part of early infantile defence mechanisms, projective identification occurs when parts of the inner world which are experienced as intolerable or unacceptable are split off and projected on to another person or object (Klein 1975). These parts may be over-idealised or denigrated, or could be understood as corresponding to that part of the self which is experienced as embodied in the picture. Bion (1977) saw projective identification not as a defence but as a mode of communication, by which the infant lets his mother know what he is feeling. Thus the feeling becomes recognised and, divested of its fear by the containing mother, is made tolerable and can be kept.

We can further understand the significance of this when looking at the work on early infancy by Esther Bick (1968). She identified the primitive basis for omnipotence as the struggle in which the young baby engages in order to survive when on his own without his mother. Her hypothesis was that the very young baby experiences the parts of its personality as having no binding force, but being held together precariously by a 'psychic skin'. The baby feels that it is in constant danger of spilling out into a state of unintegration and therefore searches for a containing object which will hold its attention. Thus the psychic skin is felt to be intact. Ultimately the containing functions of the mother are introjected and the concept of an internal space develops.

However, if the mother is absent, or present but unable to contain the baby's distress, the baby has to resort to ways of holding himself together. He is driven to act in order to survive and to defend against the catastrophic fear of a state of unintegration. If the mother cannot contain his intolerable projections, the experience is like a 'psychic hole', like a wound in the emotional skin, and the infant fears his feelings will pour out through the skin. Bick emphasised the struggle to live underlying the dependency on these primitive mechanisms and this gives a deeper comprehension of the meaning of omnipotent behaviour. The perpetuation of these survival mechanisms forms a sort of armour plating around the personality, a carapace or second skin.

This is useful to us when applied to adults in therapy. Cornwell (1984) points out that adults resort to the same survival acts in an attempt to hold themselves together. 'It has become apparent to me that children and adults in analysis are carrying out these same sorts of survival mechanisms over and over again at times of crisis' (Cornwell 1984: 4). The ways of coping are the same as for young infants, as these are felt to be familiar and safe and trustworthy. The mechanisms thus become part of the character structure as the person comes to believe that he has to do everything for himself. Therefore, it is difficult for anyone to get through to the fragility underneath.

> To conclude, I believe that this primitive fear of the state of unintegration underlies the fear of being dependent; that to experience infantile feelings of helplessness, brings back echoes of that very early unheld precariousness, and this in turn motivates the client to do it himself. At first this is done as a desperate survival measure. Gradually these defence mechanisms become built into character. Some will lead on to socially adaptive behaviour and special skills, others will remain as the basis on which other omnipotent defence mechanisms are superimposed, which further block emotional development.
>
> (Cornwell 1984: 11)

This helps us to clarify Kim's real difficulties and how he has responded to his crisis. We can also understand how crucially important is the therapist's ability to contain Kim's intolerable feelings. The image also has this function. Interestingly, the cocoon-like image actually suggests swaddling clothes, protective layers, like a 'second skin' and aspects of the cocoon convey the same precarious balance of survival between life and death, safety and danger, holding in and letting out. By expressing the intense feelings so effectively, communication is made and responded to by the therapist.

Gabrielle understood the depth of feeling that was embodied in the image. The therapist questions in her own mind what she feels is happening, and this provides a thinking space and, in the dialogue in therapy, this enables a subsequent thinking space for the client. This is like the containing function of mother which is introjected and this furthers the concept of an internal space which we saw developing in the previous image (Figure 5). Kim is consumed by despair and strong feelings of unhappiness and the therapist is holding on to the thinking for him. As the potential space in their relationship does not develop as a painting space as in some art therapy relationships, she is offering a mental space in which the completed images are explored. Interestingly, in this case the uncompleted image lacks a head but the therapist symbolically 'outlines' the head by creating the psychic space for thinking.

The ambiguities in the image and the simultaneous holding of opposites are all aspects of the complexities of Kim's experience and how he is struggling to convey it. The fact it had no head caused Kim much concern but it also enabled him to tolerate this uncertainty and ambiguity which was a difficult experience for him. The unfinished image might have been equivalent to the possibility of breaking the 'second skin' and there is the impression that it is equally devastating in his mind. This sense of devastation is also present when the picture loses its magical quality in his realisation that it will not be a candidate for the wall. Having invested the image with such magical powers, there is a tangible sense of disappointment, even deflation as if something has burst. The picture is 'inflated' in his mind and is given an aura which transcends its actual concrete existence (Schaverien 1992). This 'inflation' might also mirror some inflated sense of false self and his subsequent realisation that this is very precarious in his experience of what he really feels like. His excitement about the picture going on the wall seems to relate to some need for recognition and adoration, with his making the connection in his mind that it would give him some fame. The sexual implications of this 'four-letter word', as he describes it, give us an indication of how sexual excitement, recognition and fame are interconnected. These are demonstrated and potentially gratified by exhibiting his work and himself in this way and this highlights the primary narcissism, an early ego defence mechanism. Freud (1914) first used the term narcissism in identifying the fact that the whole of the libido is transferred onto the person himself as his only sexual object. Later analysts, such as Kohut (1972), use a wider definition, which has already been explained in Chapter 2 and has particular relevance to us in this case. There is a sense that Kim is really looking for Gabrielle's empathetic response to his 'exhibitionistic' image of himself. In Kohut's view this is central to therapeutic change.

This is important here as the theme of re-birth, metamorphosis and change is not all communicated by words but remains in the content of the image and in how he chooses to display this. He has thoughts of displaying his picture himself as an internal wish, but suddenly, in the outer world, this does not become a reality for him. Somehow Kim is making internal changes and describes strong internal feelings which need outer protection and the therapist becomes aware of this. There seems to be a connection to making the images at home where some process was taking place away from the outer world of the session. This has the effect of marking a symbolic separation from mother/therapist but there is also the sense that this identifies the creation of a potential space between Kim and mother/therapist in order that creative play and growth can occur. Winnicott (1981) informs us of this essential part of the mother–child relationship in which risks are taken and trust is established to enable this to happen. Mother holds the potential space for the child to grow and explore, create and play, and we see in this process how Kim might have been denied this experience by his mother who was too intrusive with her needs. Subsequently, there is a sense that the therapist can compensate for this by encouraging the transitional space to occur outside the session, as perhaps it feels too precarious for this to occur within the confines of the therapy room. There is risk in any play, as this involves unpredictability, and making the images at home allows Kim to create his own space in which he can begin to consolidate his emotions.

From Kim's description of making the image, we can see how he was able to play and take risks and let the process take over. Gabrielle saw the process of colouring as an activity which held significance – being able to enjoy it, become playful and become less controlling of the process and his feelings. This aspect of play and childlike exploration was an indication that creative growth was taking place, as in the potential space between mother and child. It is also clearly described by Kim. Colouring is an interesting activity when considered therapeutically, as it can be a potentially cathartic experience as defences are eroded and inner feelings emerge to the surface. Conversely, colouring in can be understood to be blotting out, filling in, covering up. Once again the image expressed this ambiguity and the possibility of holding opposites. There is some consolidation going on in the protection of the cocoon, but at the same time this might be an indication of a move away from the therapist/mother, a break from the fusion and potential separation in the building of structures for a healthy ego base.

By working so closely with the image we can see clearly how the transference is held in the image and at this stage this is where the focus remains. The transference relation shifts, as the therapist also becomes the teacher. Kim relates to the memory of the art lesson and this generates strong feelings although the anticipation of excitement is tinged with his fear of being judged. The therapist is not in touch with this stage, except to wonder whether she is the 'embalmed' mummy and takes it up in terms of compliance and his need to be worthy of treatment. By maintaining Gabrielle in an idealised state he could remain in the position of hopelessness and feeling no good. By pointing to certain qualities in the picture and accepting it, the therapist regulates both aspects – of deflation and inflation. Kim could begin to see both aspects of himself were acceptable and in this way strengthen him.

It is possible that this has made the therapeutic process tolerable for Kim, as the overwhelming nature of the interpersonal transference was terrifying for him. He expressed fears of being invaded, swamped and in despair. The image can express this for him and thus makes it bearable. He has made a symbolic safe space for himself but this can be shared with the therapist and is not an isolating experience. Winnicott (1958) points out the difference between isolation and insulation and the capacity to tolerate one without the other. The image seems to suggest that Kim is becoming aware of this in his mind. The image makes it possible to deal with these feelings as the differentiation is communicated and understood and therefore Kim can begin to make sense of them. The feelings are thus contained and do not provoke the hostile reaction that might precipitate the breakdown of therapy. The image absorbs, contains and also communicates and symbolises the intense experience that Kim is going through and in this sense is the most important vehicle for this communication. Once again it can be seen how images can hold on to feelings in a different way which can facilitate the process of working through.

Figure 7 Breaking out.

Chapter 8

Breaking out

KIM'S ACCOUNT

In our conversations, my fear of meeting people had been recognised and Gabrielle had suggested that I try to go out, to mix with people. She said that I might find a lot of my fears were unfounded; how did I know that other people would think me shallow or laugh at me? Maybe they had feelings of insecurity too. Well if they had they never showed it. I believed most people to be full of their own self-importance and over-inflated egos. I had no desire to mix with people after managing to extricate myself from them. But I still wanted to get back to being the way I was, and during my hermit-like existence I had come to realise that we are who we are in relation to the people around us. It is relationships that define our character . . . on our own we are nothing. Slowly I began to accept that I needed to take some tentative steps back into the world of socialising, not as somebody else but as myself. I remember feeling anxious, nervous and extremely vulnerable. I was uncertain of how I should speak or act, the only things that seemed to come to mind were the clichés heard on television or radio. I had spent so long pretending to be other people that I did not even know how I should look. I felt naked as if every action or word exposed my wretched soul and I had no idea how, or even less desire, to be myself – Mr Nobody.

To go out among people who seemed to think so much of themselves (too much in my opinion considering that they were not famous pop stars) I needed something to bolster my confidence, a bit of an image to put to people. So I still took up a rock'n'roll image, albeit more ambiguous: no one in particular, just black jeans and a biker's jacket. I bought these bearing in mind I was returning to college and knowing I would stick out like a sore thumb (by virtue of my age). I felt I needed to look tough or at least tougher than I felt.

With this sort of image I went to a party of some old friends of mine whom I had not seen socially for quite some time. I had been turning down invitations using my portfolio preparation as an excuse. They were pleased to see me, overly so it seemed to me, and this made me a little uneasy.

How much did they know about my problems? Had they guessed the real reason why I had been hiding myself away? I tried not to get paranoid about this and did my best to relax and be myself; consequently I did not have a lot to say and started to feel left out. I did not know how to join in, I was on the outside watching still, as I ever was, so I left early, not feeling particularly happy with myself. Yes I had gone out, yes I had not pretended to be anyone else, but I was no nearer to being myself or who I used to be. Old habits die hard. I was disappointed and I remember, on the bus journey home, watching people being themselves in pub gardens, on café verandas, in restaurant windows, on their way to a club perhaps or even in their own homes. They were just being themselves which wasn't so wonderful, but they were enjoying themselves. And I was not.

This picture was done around that time – it is not really meant to be heroic, like a phoenix rising from the flames, though that is how it may appear at first. The flames at the bottom of the picture are meant to represent the hell of the past from which I was emerging. To be honest the mass of green at the top has no less symbolic value than the fact that, as a contender for the 'wall' (and I had already decided that this was going to be the one), I felt I needed to cover the paper with medium instead of leaving a lot of blank paper around the image as I had done previously. However, I did have a reason for choosing green and that was that I had read somewhere that green is often associated with growth, not just the plants at springtime but also the spiritual kind. This image may tie in with the sort of heroic aspect and powers that I was trying to endow the 'Harlequin' with. In the picture I am tearing open the shell or cocoon with my bare hands. This cocoon was in reality more like a suit of armour. This armour was the various images of the other people I had pretended to be in the past, when I modified my behaviour to mimic whichever pop star I wanted to be at that time. Not only that but thinking how they would react or speak in a certain situation had become first nature to me.

Through being other people for so long my thoughts on how I should be were replaced with how I wanted to be and act (like them). This meant I experienced nothing of the world around me 'first hand' which, when I considered the world to be such an awful place, was not a bad thing. In reality however, I certainly wasn't feeling as strong as I depicted myself, far from it, and looking back I can see how I was visualising a strength (and power) that I didn't have, but wished I had as a way of boosting my confidence and ego.

My obsession with image still got the better of me as I used a silver marker pen for the zips and studs on the biker's jacket. I kidded myself that a 'mixed media' picture was a good enough excuse if Gabrielle had pointed this detail out. I was a little concerned about taking this picture along to Gabrielle, that she would say that I was still clinging to image too much. I mean you can see it, just exchanging the old for a new one, but

I was grateful she did not mention this and I believed that she indulged me because she believed it was good for my confidence. She commented on all the positive aspects of the picture; indeed there are no negative ones, in particular the strength I am displaying – see how the shell is buckling in the grip of my right hand. Gabrielle asked how I felt about putting this picture on the wall. I was very pleased, I felt as if I had achieved something.

THERAPIST'S RESPONSE

In the preceding picture, Kim had drawn the cocoon. This had simultaneously represented Kim both wrapping himself tightly in place as a protection and a burst of colour within the cocoon. This picture follows on, since it is Kim's attempt to break through some of these outer layers, to discover what may lie beneath the surface. While, on first impression this may be seen as quite a contrived image, there is an honesty and coherence to it. It may be seen to reflect Kim's struggle to keep everything in place that was known and familiar to him, and his desire to break this fragile shell, that had recently caused him so much pain. As such, the picture was a metaphor for his struggle to break down some of his external mask in a search for his own identity in an attempt to find a 'real self'.

He described this picture as his breaking through a suit of armour. Kim had drawn the suit of armour, broken through the middle with a figure emerging from it. The armour had been cracked rather like the shell of an egg. Left behind, discarded, are two muscular-looking sides of armour with two unknown heads and bodies. The figure pushing aside the armour is dressed in a fashionable leather jacket covered in studs, chains and a belt. The face had a chiselled sculptured look, as if it had been created. Although the features are not recognisable as Kim, the face made me wonder how Kim's face looks when he constructs a new mask for himself.

Kim was to describe the field of flames in which the man is standing as the hell from which he was emerging. I wondered with him whether the fire would melt the suit of armour or burn the figure inside. Although Kim did not at the time know the answer to such a question my aim was to establish that there was more than one way to make sense of his dreams, pictures, reveries. Until now his internal representations encouraged him to have a frame of reference for himself that would ultimately involve some form of self-destruction. I felt one of our aims was to open up possibilities which ultimately would lead to Kim having a sense that he had some real choices.

We discussed the picture together and Kim said how pleased he was in the making of it. He felt the suit of armour was an important symbolic leap for him and he was able to recognise that behind the armour was another cocoon, another mask to get behind. The picture reminded me of

Russian dolls, making the link between the outset of Kim's process of taking off his external layers and these beautiful bright painted dolls which are enclosed inside one another. As the outer layers are opened there is another one inside until the final doll is opened and there is nothing left. We talked about the idea of discovering that there is nothing inside and the anxiety about this. The masks protected him against the discovery of finding what was inside: the fear of finding nothing. In this way Kim had found a way of communicating his struggle to describe the protective shields he had built up over the years. I sensed that there was some shame, some embarrassment that he had presented me with, in his eyes, another false persona. I picked up that Kim expected me to criticise him for not achieving a greater honesty by being able to reach a genuine and authentic part of himself. His expectation that I would see the picture critically no doubt reflected an earlier template in his life, but I chose not to take it up in the transference in this way, rather to acknowledge that this image was a powerful communication to both Kim and myself. It reflected his genuine struggle to break through these layers, his defence structure; an attempt to uncover the protective masks he had built up over the years, but he needed to find his own pace to do this and I felt the need to respect this.

My feeling was that the dismantling of himself was beginning to make him feel profoundly depleted. While Kim deeply held this fear, he was also communicating to me that making the images could help him survive these overwhelming feelings. In his urgency to find another way of living, he had also demonstrated that he was tentatively setting the foundations of a real relationship with me which he would be able to translate to the world outside.

This became clearer to me as this picture was to act as a catalyst for the exploration of his relationship with his girlfriend which had ended two years prior to coming into therapy. In a previous image, he had drawn himself sitting in a restaurant with his girlfriend. Discarded on the floor was a suit of armour lying in a heap. Kim described how she had confronted him about his mask he had been presenting to the outside world. She had suggested that she would prefer him without the mask and wanted him to show her more of the real Kim. As Kim began to absorb this idea and began to let down his mask, he described how it had left him feeling empty and hollow with little or no sense of self. The consequences were initially devastating for him and were to set the foundations for his profound depression and the crisis that had led him to therapy.

It was his connection to this experience that formed the basis for a powerful series of pictures in which he attempted to represent his struggle to break through his suit of armour and find what was on the inside. He described how this had been his only relationship and it had left him feeling humiliated and depleted. He felt emotionally bruised. It was as if he had lost his protective shield and that he was left empty inside.

What I felt was emerging was the sense that when his external persona was unmasked it left him feeling passive and vulnerable. He had no sense of self that allowed him to stand as a separate person. It became apparent that it seemed important for Kim to allow himself to explore the meaning of the relationship with Sam. Kim described how in the early days of the relationship, he had been instrumental in enabling Sam to develop herself. He had helped with her application to art school, which was successful, leaving him feeling useless and a failure. Kim felt unable to explore any of these angry, envious emotions that surrounded this experience. He was to internalise them, turning them against himself, which contributed to his depression.

This was Kim's first sexual relationship. Previously, relationships with girls had been to have pretty girls for adornment not intimacy. Although he was able to experience some satisfaction in this relationship at first, he described how it quickly went wrong. He talked about feeling engulfed and overwhelmed. He became terrified of losing himself, not existing. He became frozen, fearful of the relationship and for him it fulfilled his worst fears.

At the time, Kim had not understood what had happened between them and why it went wrong and how his earlier significant relationships, for example with parental figures, had influenced his experience. What he had internalised and communicated to me was that he was wretched, had nothing to offer and was the destructive partner. In his mind it was him who had spoiled things. By gradually beginning to talk about these experiences as a result of making the image, he no longer felt so consumed with guilt and a sense of his own inadequacy.

It seemed to me that many of his fears of being overwhelmed and swamped were associated with earlier relationships. Kim had spoken about these same emotions in relationship to his mother. It seemed important that he could differentiate himself from his mother, which would allow him a separate sense of who he was. His attempts to differentiate and separate himself from his family experience became clearer when he acknowledged his attraction to and preference for non-white women. He mentioned the fact that his idol had a girlfriend of mixed race. When I pointed out some links between the relationship with his girlfriend and that with his mother, he felt able to challenge these associations and this began the process of being able to differentiate himself from me. The fact that he was now able to question what I said and not always compliantly accept it was an important development in our relationship and necessary in working through the idealisation, which was beginning to shift. He could initiate some foundations of feeling less merged with me and of the establishment of his own sense of separateness. I felt able to make these links because he was now demonstrating a capacity to take this in and I was responding to the notion of readiness.

It was at this point that I asked Kim if he felt ready to choose one of his pictures to put on the wall and it was this image he chose. As part of my working practice I ask clients to select a picture. Such practice is controversial within the art therapy profession. For me it serves several therapeutic functions. Critical to the process is the state of readiness and the person with whom I am working feeling able to move from the image being a private one to being a public one. This process often diminishes the intensity of the image and makes it less overwhelming to the client. It is perhaps also a symbolic way of them making a permanent mark in the art therapy space. Some clients link this with feelings of validation and being taken seriously. For someone who has a very faint sense of self, it can be a powerful external expression. I choose to frame each picture carefully. This very activity further reinforces the idea of being taken seriously. It is as if they now have a mark or influence on the therapist or institution. It serves to help diminish the unequal power relationship: where they are 'being influenced', they can now influence me and other clients. The presence of the picture acts as a catalyst for other clients' experience, not however in an intrusive way, as the client can choose how far he or she engages, responds to or even notices the pictures of other people. At first when I framed Kim's picture he seemed embarrassed and shy. He acknowledged he had never framed one of his own pictures because he did not think they were worth it. I felt that he did not take himself sufficiently seriously to believe that someone else would but he was pleased with the picture and this is why he chose it. To me it felt like a consolidatory experience.

OVERVIEW

It is noticeable at this stage of the process how Kim is now able to make use of the voice of the image to express his real self. This image is a clear statement about how he feels and in this sense speaks for itself. His own description clearly demonstrates the essence of his struggle to understand and be understood. It is interesting that he feels it must be 'acceptable', that is that Gabrielle will be able to relate to the picture first, before he is able to explore it. In this way, the picture represents his self-image which must on the surface be acceptable. She senses that he is expecting a critical response but does not take this up. This focuses the initial anxiety of acceptance and acceptability which is projected onto the image and the image therefore is empowered to speak for him in this way.

The image has associations of a phoenix rising out of ashes, something is appearing as if out of nothing, which enables the therapist to encourage Kim to look into this. There is a clarity about the work which suggests some need inside Kim to do this and marks some tentative beginnings towards individuation. The image contains harmony and balance which seems poised in spite of being violently cracked open. It is static and active at the same time, perhaps reflecting the real ambivalence about change and growth. The figure is somewhat sexually ambiguous which suggests that this is part of Kim's struggle for understanding of himself. However, it is full of strength and energy with a head which is looking outwardly.

What seems to become evident to both therapist and client is the strong communication of the false persona that is emerging in the picture and is therefore beginning to break down. The masks hide the masks but he was beginning to be able to enable the important links to break through this. The fire in which the figure is situated raises the question of whether the figure is being melted down or destroyed or whether he is perched on the edge of both. Kim describes this as emerging out of the hell of the past but equally the image suggests the hell of the emptiness or 'non-identity'. There is even mention of feeling transparent – that people can 'see' inside Kim and his real problems. The therapist notices this and this confirms her sense that communications are more open and that important issues are surfacing. The art therapist, who is familiar with the subtleties of image making, is skilled in perceiving this in the images and can work with it accordingly. What is interesting is how this session proceeds as a result.

Kim describes the break-up of his relationship with his girlfriend and for the first time seems able to explore this, his feelings about it and the implications for him now. The therapist is in touch with his dilemma and picks up on his capacity to be open about his feelings but acknowledges the risk he takes in talking about relationships with others which in the past have caused him so much difficulty. This is made clear in the therapist's remarks about previous relationships and Kim's response in which he is beginning to risk questioning the therapist and have a non-compliant attitude towards her. He can begin to risk and acknowledge some angry feelings. At the same time he perceives Gabrielle as 'helping him' and 'indulging' him with compliments, when in fact Gabrielle has a different experience. She feels that he cannot take in anything to validate his experience and so is intent on 'rubbishing' it.

There is a very interesting discrepancy here between Gabrielle's recognition and valuing of the image, which she does by taking it seriously and trying to understand its communication, and Kim's experience of this communication as flattery to make him feel better. If, however, we look underneath the surface we see how the transference relationship is at work. Kim expects Gabrielle to humiliate him which is a measure of some of his earlier experiences. He expects to be made a fool of. He feels unworthy of an authentic communication, he cannot allow himself to take it in. While Gabrielle has valued his ability to make a powerful visual image, he cannot allow himself to experience this as real. As yet, he is not in touch with his true self but a defensive adaptation that has learnt to 'rubbish' everything.

Orbach and Eichenbaum (1993) state that the therapist's words are 'not a reparative response to what was lacking but an authentic spontaneous appreciation transcending earlier dynamics'. Critical to the process of change is Gabrielle's understanding of the need to hold the genuineness of her response available until Kim is able to digest it in a new and different way. 'Therapy proceeds not so much by virtue of the therapist's capacity to provide the client with de nova experiences, as by her capacity to resist being converted into old and familiar experiences' (Levenson 1991). We can see how central the use of the image is in containing the emotional content of the interaction until Kim is ready to take it in in some palatable form.

This becomes clearer as Kim begins to explore his previous relationships. We see how he is able to explore different fantasies of female love objects and this is talked about in terms of his attraction to particular women. This may be an indication of his struggle with his emerging feelings towards the therapist as a woman. As the therapist becomes a sexual object, the transference shifts to a more sexualised base. As a result the therapist is also able to experience him as more separate. There is a sense that these sexual feelings are still masked and, at this point, the therapist introduces the idea of the Russian dolls which are wooden, repeating but diminishing female objects. We must consider here the counter-transference response of the therapist when she introduces this as, although, on one level, she is responding to the fear of emptiness and what is inside or behind the masks, this is also perhaps her way of responding to this shift and the emergence of strong feelings towards her.

However, the introduction of the image of the dolls does focus on the central problem of Kim's intense anxiety about having nothing inside. The ambivalence of wanting to find out but fearing what he might find is highlighted and thus the paradoxical situation is communicated. It seems to consist of a sense of extreme weakness and vulnerability combined with its exact opposite, a sense of superiority and potential if not actual omnipotence. Milner (1987) describes the state of omnipotence and omniscience of thought as a protection against impotence and lack of capacity to control. Kim talks about seeming to have power and potency but there is also an anxiety that he is transparent. This combination of opposites seems to originate from a self-perception that Kim is a helpless person but at the same time omnipotent.

We can see why Kim is so strongly connected to Gabrielle's opinion. His primary need is that he will be accepted by her. If there is emptiness in his portrayal of himself, there is the possibility of filling up which seems to be a strong aspect of their relationship. He can now experience Gabrielle as a fulfilling object who is not draining or emptying but nurturing and restoring. The need to 'fill up' the space on the picture might have some connection to this unconscious process that is emerging. It is interesting how this becomes manifest in the exploration of the picture. The image suggests pushing out, forceful development, the struggle of birth which suggests possibilities of a vacuum – a vulnerable defenceless state.

Babies are born helpless and vulnerable, and gradually confidence and a sense of security is acquired when basic needs are met by mother. This develops a basic sense of trust. But, if these needs are not met, a basic sense of mistrust is likely to develop, which makes it dangerous to become emotionally involved and relationships become connected to risk and anxiety. This is how the need to keep people at arm's length, to avoid close personal contact, and 'wearing a mask' develops, as playing roles becomes the appropriate way to relate, which hides the real feelings inside. In this way it is possible to understand how the sense of inferiority and omnipotence can coexist, as real feelings or the real self is hidden by the 'false self'. One is reminded of Winnicott's famous remark in his paper 'On Communication': 'In the artist of all kinds, I think one can detect an inherent dilemma which belongs to the co-existence of two trends, the urgent need to communicate and the still more urgent need not to be found' (Winnicott 1963: 185). The image speaks directly of this.

This way of thinking is useful for us to understand what is at the root of Kim's fears. The central fear is that of finding nothing inside. He is in touch with the futility of his existence. Many writers comment on this primitive anxiety (Fairbairn 1952) and others give us some understanding as to how creative activity is used to cope with these feelings (Milner 1987; Segal 1975; Segal 1957). For example, Storr (1972) feels that as the artist strives to create to defend against the threat of finding the world meaningless this forms the foundations of creativity. As an activity it is solitary, does not require anyone else or any emotional contact; it maintains the phantasy of omnipotence and offers the opportunity for others to emulate the artist. A sense of control is maintained by cutting down unpredictable or arbitrary events, thus the artist feels he is in control of his own world. This is easier to manage than the complexity of relationships in the outside world.

Kim is beginning to understand that relationships are important even though this requires him to become separate, someone in his own right. Interaction between people provides meaning and significance in life while creative activity can act as an alternative. These developments in thinking are commented on directly by Kim. Here there is evidence of an internal shift as indicated by his understanding of this picture and this informs the therapist who is holding in mind the 'the notion of readiness'. The therapist is clear in pointing out that in her view Kim is reaching that stage in which there is a capacity to take things in, to internalise and therefore make some internal shifts. With the removal of his outer shell, which is so graphically described in the image, the exposed inside can allow an interchange both in and out and thus ambivalent and conflicting feelings can be felt and tolerated. Interestingly, the same notion of readiness is also present when Kim is asked whether he is ready to make a public statement about his pictures. It is noticeable how these coincide in the same session and this demonstrates how the processes are communicated and are connected together in the therapist's mind.

Kim also came with the same thoughts and he was 'ready' for his picture to be displayed. He had thought about how to justify the image and once again we see the link between the picture and his self-image. Underneath, Kim feared Gabrielle's attack, that the image might be empty, and he makes a conscious connection to this, perhaps to protect himself and his own feelings of emptiness. We see how he can use the materials 'defensively' in his choice to fill up the space, to defend against the possibility of emptiness by covering it up with green. Kim associates this with growth but it could also be connected to his envious feelings of how he sees the successful other. This image preparation can be seen to be a strengthening experience, it is containing, confirming and, for Kim, it is important for the process in his relationship with the image, his own self-image and the therapist. She affirms his picture making which affirms his tentative, vulnerable self-image.

Gabrielle describes this as her particular way of working and the reasons why she chooses to do this. This is built into her working style but it is not always the practice among art therapists. The debate about putting clients' pictures on the wall continues among the art therapy profession and the advantages and disadvantages are useful to consider. Publicly displaying them in the art room, where they are made, with the clients' active choice and consent, gives them a specialness, value and the statement that this is important. They are owned by the person and yet anonymous to the public and so indicate that there was a special relationship in the making. They act as a personal container that can withstand the intrusion of the public gaze and aesthetic response. The difficulties lie in the aspects of confidentiality and exposure that are put at risk. The effect on the other clients using the room can be valuable if there is projective material that can be used in the work, but pictures can be frightening and disturbing for others or even overwhelming and may stop the process of a session. For example, if a group or individual is in the room there can be a very strong response to the images on the walls in terms of the therapeutic process and what subsequently surfaces and is made conscious. The therapist must be able to work skilfully to make interpretations that can use this material and not allow the resonance from the image to become a destructive or persecutory force. Images on the wall are strong statements and many therapists feel pictures should be kept privately in the safe-keeping of a folder until the end of treatment. Others work with a more open attitude to the images produced and work within the scope of using the walls for space and safe-keeping of the image. This is an interesting dilemma, often depending on the particular client group, but should always be thought through in working practice.

What is most interesting, in terms of this particular process, is that the 'wall' has been a central dynamic in this therapeutic relationship right from the first session. The link with the Harlequin image is useful in that Kim could now make up for his disappointment by this next image being 'chosen'. This also reminds us of the idea of the cocoon changing into something else, shedding its skin within the process of metamorphosis. The discarded armour in the image was a sign that perhaps the layers were ready to be taken off, and, to some extent, being able to leave this picture on the wall seems to symbolise the same process. The image is placed on the wall, like the discarded armour or the dead skin. It has been useful and active while it was needed for the process of working through but now it is perceived to have a different function and can be preserved. The image or the outer skin or armour has served its purpose. It is possible to leave this, with the understanding of it as some important aspect of self within the safe-keeping of the therapy room. It remains separate from Kim as he can leave behind and discard this protective layer.

Figure 8 Against the tide.

Chapter 9

Search for identity

KIM'S ACCOUNT

There was another fear as well that made me reluctant to go among people – to socialise. I saw people en masse, moving as a homogeneous whole, going about their daily routine of working and then, to make up for the fact that they did not like their work, socialising. My worry about socialising was that I would become part of this mass of humanity which I detested, with no real goals in life and just drifting along. I did not want to be a part of that, there had to be a point in my life. I didn't know what, but I had taken a stab at it by deciding to be a designer and I was going to do my damnedest to be the best I could and this would not allow any time for socialising.

Another thought occurred to me. If and when I did find myself, I might turn out to be as boring as I feared, as boring as everybody else. I would find my identity only to lose it. But Gabrielle helped me think about the possibility of mixing with other people and I was starting to accept that living 'alone' was not wholly healthy for me.

I tried to illustrate how I felt about the idea of going among people, and there I am amidst a sea of faceless people or 'nobodies'. They are all walking mindlessly forward within the confines of two tall walls. It is me who is rising above the mass, my arm raised towards the coloured sky which nobody else seems aware of. From my hand radiate bright rays of light which I imagined emanating from some kind of magical ring I might be wearing. The light was not necessarily meant to be like a beacon to 'show the way' though I see now how it might appear so. At the time the light was my light, which I am holding aloft to make me stand out from the crowd, to distinguish me and state 'look I am here'. But the others do not see it, they are blinkered and just keep marching along. The walls are too high to climb so I cannot go sideways, going back (against the tide) is very difficult if not impossible, what can I do? I am caught in the flow.

I was disappointed with the end result of this picture. It did not convey the extent of my fear of being lost in the crowd. My token 'masses' represent just a small fraction of all the people who go through the same motions in their lives, and the end result of the image does not show much hope for me in fighting against this almost inevitable end, should I decide to go among them.

Gabrielle could see this picture as me being lost in the crowd but it was not clear to her that I was trying to go back. When I pointed this out, she reminded me that I was struggling with going back to what I knew, and I told her of my fears of going forward. You see, when you are depressed the way forward is not just unclear, it is frightening. Your lack of confidence and self-esteem impairs your judgement and you become unsure about being able to make the right decisions. After all, you must have made so many wrong ones to have got into the mess. How can you possibly trust yourself to make the right ones now? You just don't know.

And when you start to get better and have to face the future and be responsible for your actions, because you can no longer blame them on your illness, there is a temptation to go back into your despair where you can hide from the realities of the world. And the path back is very familiar and clear, you just have to look over your shoulder and there it is, every inch that you have built on the way out of your depression. When you look ahead, the path stops at your toes, it doesn't exist any further because you haven't built it yet.

So you are stuck, and even though you have the most awful feelings of being lost or in limbo, it would be a comfort to stay where you are, knowing that you have made some progress but can still use your illness as an excuse for your failures. I was frightened by a future where I could not blame depression for my mess. Gabrielle was able to recognise some of these feelings, and my struggle to reach the light and how this might present a way out for me. In the picture I did not seem to be lost in the crowd and perhaps I had the strength to rise above it. Not only that but the light shining from me shows that I do have something to offer, and if I go out and meet people I might have a different experience to the one I anticipate.

I had been doing self-portraits on a regular basis for over a year, under cover of my portfolio presentation. At one interview in particular (the college at which I was later to get a place) I was asked by the tutors why I had done so many. One of them suggested it might be vanity (this was worrying – maybe it was), but the other remarked that most well-known artists have a string of self-portraits to their name (I took this as a compliment at the time – but maybe he was being sarcastic). I protested that I was endeavouring to improve my drawing skills and experiment with different media, therefore it was important to have a constant subject. This was not wholly true.

Yes, I wanted them to see my newly acquired skills in drawing and painting but these pictures were more than just practice to me. At the time of their execution I wanted them to show something about THAT time in my life, a record of my suffering. In retrospect I can see that it was not wise to present this sort of work when trying to get a place on a college course. After all, who wants a manic-depressive in their class? With these pictures in addition to the problems I was having in 'putting on a brave face', it was no wonder that I had so much trouble being accepted.

The portrait shown in Figure 9 was done on the Saturday evening that I moved into my lodgings near the college where I was due to start that Monday. I wanted a record of this point in my life where I was starting all over again, and not just educationally. I had a lot of self-doubts at that time and Gabrielle had been very supportive. When I first secured the place on a course I had new problems. . . . Where would I live and would I be able to manage it this time? I was sure that I was going to end up in some dingy little room, and that would not be good for my state of mind. Gabrielle asked me to try and imagine a better outcome. I might not end up in such a bad situation after all and, as luck would have it, I found lodgings in a very nice house indeed. As far as supporting myself went I believed I would end up working in a fast food restaurant and having to wear one of those awful uniforms and silly hats would not just have been degrading but also a blow to the construction of my new identity – or was it vanity again? After asking around in the High Street I found a Saturday job as a staff supervisor in a shoe shop and that was not so bad. I had to wear black trousers, a white shirt and a tie, clothes that were familiar to me.

The fears and doubts I had at the time were in some way balanced by the fact that after a year of trying, I had finally achieved the first step I needed to start rebuilding my life, which I never really expected to happen because I had become so used to disappointments. Nevertheless I still had anxieties. I was joining a class of thirty people whom I did not know. Some of them would have the advantage of knowing each other. I believed they would all be 'full of themselves' due to their young age, and confident because they had already gained a lower-grade graphic design qualification, whereas the reason I had been accepted was, as the tutors told me, that they were impressed that I had actually come back a year later after being initially refused. Usually people give up and they never see them again. I was lacking in knowledge and experience compared to the rest of the class and, though I was prepared to work hard and catch up, I knew I would be disadvantaged initially. The only advantage I had over them was my age. I was approximately eight years older than the class and I thought I could use this to distance myself from them until I felt more able to cope with associating with them. The fear of failure was still with me of course. Would I be able to 'cut it'? To fail in the company of younger people would be very embarrassing indeed, and, when I thought about it, the fact I was older meant that I should be better than them, so I started the course believing that I had to be the best. I had to show them. It was this pressure that I put upon myself from the outset that was my main motivation for doing well.

This portrait is one of my favourites because it was a breakthrough. It was the most realistic/human one I had done. Up till then I had been using pencil and watercolours trying to create a likeness through an obsession with detail. Those pictures had an unreal quality. For this picture however I used conte crayons because Gabrielle suggested I needed a medium to help me loosen up and get some expression onto the paper. I decided to work on black paper and built up my face by showing light rather than working on white and using shadow. This way the face looks as if it is appearing out of the surface of the paper. It was a good likeness, there is something melancholic about it and it looks fragile. It was me. This is also

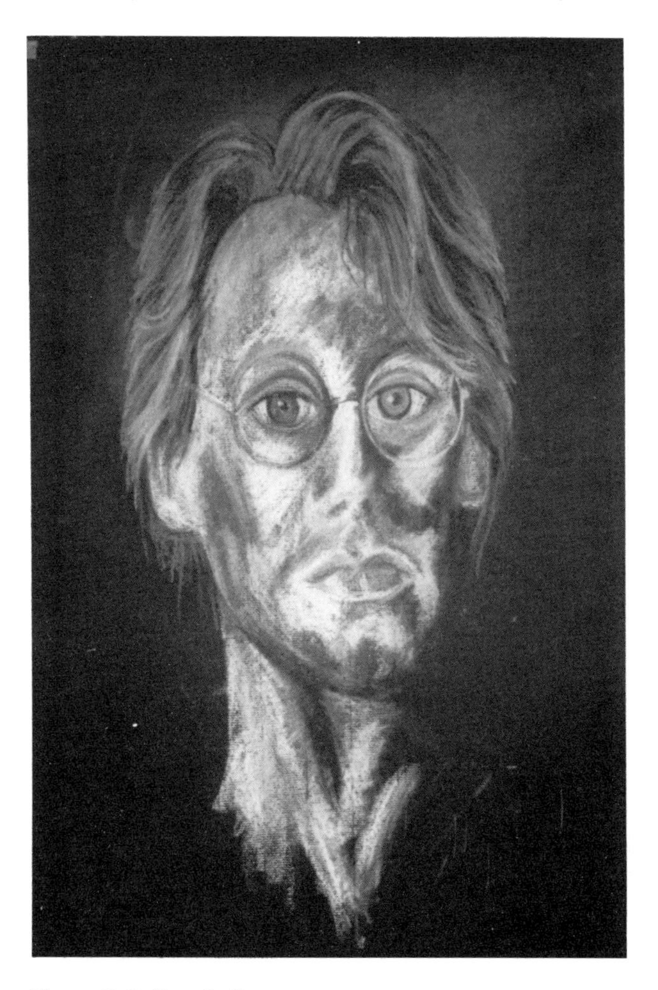

Figure 9 Self-portrait.

the only picture I have drawn of myself with my glasses on. I believe that, because I was starting college, I wanted to show myself as an intellectual. Maybe I was once again trying to endow myself with properties I didn't think I had through my pictures.

THERAPIST'S RESPONSE

As Kim was to remove his false persona, he began to struggle with who he was, both on the inside and on the outside. He came to understand that for several years he had developed a very elaborate disguise whereby he was well defended against people getting to know who he really was. Kim came to share with me how this presentation of himself went back to when he was at secondary school. Even there he had established a very sophisticated persona, whereby he was idolising a famous pop star. He started to dye and perm his hair, wear foundation on his face and eye-shadow. His wardrobe was a replication of the pop star's. He even went to his tailor on Great Marlborough Street. He had a wardrobe of stage jackets that were a direct imitation. Kim described how he had become a 'legend in his lunchbreak' and thus was idealised as a star at school. While there were clearly some positive aspects for Kim in the development of this persona, it was to serve to distance himself and others further from the Kim that thought, felt and had genuine emotions. While such a mask would attract attention, people were not to relate to him as Kim, but to his mask.

I got the feeling that this elaborate charade served him fairly well as a device, probably unconscious at the time, to prevent him feeling swamped and overwhelmed by his feelings. It may have also served him as a means of creating a distance between him and his family. His mask enabled him to be somebody else, which is what he wanted. It was as if he had programmed himself to think and feel like another person. Being Kim was too difficult.

This complex reconstruction of himself was to serve him well for a number of years until he became severely ill with ulcerated colitis at the age of eighteen. This involved hospitalisation and a great deal of pain. At the time, he felt his family were unable to understand his experience and he felt abandoned by most of the friends he had. It seemed that Kim distanced himself from any friendships as he could not bear to let them see him vulnerable, or any part of the real inner him. He felt they would only want to know him for the pop star idol he imitated. This period of Kim's life would seem to have been one of despair. He talked about how he would wish he was dead.

This profound experience seemed to have alienated him even further from who he really was. He was to choose a new persona. This time it was a sombre character with no humour. He set about creating himself in this image. Such was the all-absorbing nature of his commitment that he would spend all his money on a wardrobe that was a replica of his idol's. The way he moved, walked, talked, sat and smoked was to ensure that he was an identical clone. He was once more all consumed by his image, his external presentation of himself to hide against the inner pain. How he looked was what he was. There was no place for feelings, emotions, frailties, vulnerability or strength. He was what he presented to the outside world. This image was to start to break down about a year before he entered therapy.

Kim made a series of pictures which explored this external presentation of himself. It clearly coincided with the internal representation of himself. What he really thought and felt was to be communicated in the twelve pictures he made which are all connected with his attempt to define a clearer sense of who he was.

This series was to coincide with Kim starting his course at college. He was acutely aware of himself in relation to the rest of the class – how they perceived him, could they see through him, was he transparent with nothing inside? Kim had been anxious and preoccupied before college started as to whether he would manage the course. Would he be much less able than the other students, would he sustain it or would he be asked to leave? Although I could already see that his artistic and creative level of competence was not in doubt, it was of little use to communicate this to Kim at the time. Such an act of reassurance would have left Kim just as depleted. He came to know this himself, with time, on the inside.

Many of Kim's immediate concerns were displaced into finding accommodation and his anxiety level at the time was extremely high. This, I thought, was related more to his fears about managing relationships and the contact demanded of him on the course rather than the practical realities of finding a room. Much of my task throughout this period was to support him in this activity and I felt it would have been little use to have interpreted his anxiety. My sense was that he needed at the time a sufficient level of containment and support to encourage him to lay down the necessary practical foundations required to find a base for himself. He was still living a hermit's existence and one of my functions, as I saw it, was to help him test reality and change the perspective of his distorted mirror, to be better prepared for the world outside.

Two images have been selected as illustrations of his struggle. The first image is 'Against the tide' (Figure 8). A crowd of charcoal figures is surging forward, densely packed together, pressing against one another, marching down a corridor. The figures have a computer-like quality, marching in time to an internal computer. The computer has been conditioned externally by the pressure from the group, not from the real sense. Out of the crowd, one figure is leaping into the air. He is differentiated from the rest by his position, his movement with his arm in the air, his more carefully formed figure and his long dark hair. The other figures, although quickly drawn, all have a sameness to them. The figure leaping into the air seems to be pointing at the burst of colour in the sky, the beautiful swirls of colour. Although carefully drawn and he has introduced colour, the colour marks are still faint, and are reminiscent of Kim's drawing of the cocoon.

This picture spoke clearly for itself. Kim's struggle not to be swamped in the crowd, lost without any identity. His profound fear that once he came out into the world again, placed himself in contact with his contemporaries, he would lose any recent gains in discovering who he was. In practice, this would mean he would be unnoticed, unremembered by those around him. He would be so insignificant that he would be a faint presence. Kim's only known response to this was such a caricature, such a loud statement that he could not fail to be noticed. Could he be recognised, responded to and related to for who he really was? The picture to me suggested the foundations of him beginning to differentiate himself. This picture was part of a series in which he was to reconstruct himself. In this picture he is reaching out to the burst of light, the colour, perhaps a symbol of his own internal creativity. The part of him that he was to internalise was to allow him to differentiate himself from the crowd, to find a real sense of who he was from his internal core.

I linked this in my mind with the notion of internal psychological space in which the capacity to separate between feelings and thinking is lost. When demands are so pressing, thinking and feeling merge and act to create internal confusion and anxiety. Hence the crowd pressing in may be a symbolic crowd. The external world becomes a frightening place since it deprives you of the possibility of feeling in some control. As Kim began to lift his head out of the crowd, it was perhaps beginning to differentiate thought from feeling, the foundations for beginning to live in a less enmeshed world.

The self-portrait (Figure 9) was one of a series that Kim was to complete. This one was done by him the evening before he was starting college. He was feeling anxious, struggling with how he was going to present himself to the tutors and his fellow students. Making a picture he now knew was a way to contain himself, reduce his anxiety and get some of the fears he had from the inside to the outside. I had recently suggested to Kim that he might try conte pastels as it might increase his sense of freedom when making a picture.

Kim selected a black piece of paper but has chosen a wide range of colours to express himself. He has drawn himself with high cheek bones, a rather gaunt aesthetic look. The face has a sober, melancholic quality, but there is a sensitivity and humanity to the picture. The previous self-portraits had been flat and lifeless; this one was more three-dimensional and perhaps represented his desire to present himself in that way. The eyes have a warmth and make contact when you look at them. Kim gave himself a pair of glasses. Kim shared with me how in the past he had been too vain to wear glasses although he needed them. I wondered if the glasses represented not only a reduction in the vanity but also a desire to see more clearly.

The picture echoed a greater consistency between how he felt about himself on the inside and how he might show himself to the outside world. It communicated a sensitivity, a humanity and a vulnerability. Kim however was still struggling in the transitional space, for although he allowed me to see the melancholic, vulnerable side of himself, he had not found a way of communicating this to anyone else. The picture was to increase Kim's awareness that he would like to show more of himself, but as yet did not know how to. He has begun to put together inner and outer worlds. He is not so intensely split, but the picture is ahead of his emotional development. There was evidence of him pretending less. We talked together about what it was like to go out without all this elaborate disguise. Each time he experimented it was to become less painful. Although he was still fearful of people seeing who he really was, he was continuing to struggle with this. He wanted to show more of his real self, but was still not quite ready to do so.

OVERVIEW

What we are seeing here is a real development in the understanding and acknowledgement of the experience of inside and outside – what are internal feelings and what belongs outside to a mask or façade. The first image is Kim lost in a crowd in which he fears he does not exist, but on the outside he has to be very different in order to survive. There is a sense that he has allowed the therapist to see inside him, to be inside him and, in this process of internalisation, he can manage without too much anxiety and fear. This experience has enabled him to think about the fear of being swallowed up, completely engulfed by people and being totally merged and fused together. The possibility of separation is emerging, the identification of 'me' and 'not me' which Winnicott (1951) describes so well. If Kim is unique and feels special and separate then the feared fusion cannot happen. The beginnings of an internal acceptance of being together without being merged is developing, as described clearly in his image. There is a way out, and he is separate, but it is tolerable to be among others. The beginnings of differentiation have occurred with the therapist, he now has to negotiate this within a group. Klein also reminds us:

> In considering from the psycho-analytic point of view the behaviour of people in their social surroundings, it is necessary to investigate how the individual develops from infancy into maturity. A group – whether large or small – consists of individuals in a relationship to one another;

> and therefore the understanding of personality is the foundation for the understanding of social life.
>
> (Klein 1959: 3)

It is interesting how many aspects of this image point to this process over time – the dolls, the cocoon, which are like outer shells or masks hiding the process within. The tunnel itself could also be a container in the same way and, as with the early framework of his family seen in Chapter 3, is this tunnel a container or a restriction? Is he struggling to burst out or feeling safe by being held in? There is a feeling that he is struggling to get out of the crowd, though he is still isolated in his life outside and so still sees people as frightening objects, as having the capacity to mow him down. His fear of joining this group of 'younger' people seems to resonate also with his experience of being the older brother. Deep down he fears the rejection of the group but equally the possibility of being caught in the same dynamic as in his family in which he felt trapped. This is his only other real experience of a group.

The image is sinister in that it conveys that he fears all the people in the crowd are hollow, empty and robotic which perhaps mirrors his own perception of himself. The experience of being in the tunnel conveys Kim's ambivalence in his feelings about proximity and closeness for which he partly longs and yet which he partly fears. The image radiates light, colour and rays of hope but these are fenced in with a squashed, dark and dingy tunnel which has a close, claustrophobic feel about it. For the first time there are other people in the picture, although an amorphous undifferentiated mass, which suggests the acknowledgement of other relationships. The real ambivalence seems to rest in his longing for, but fear of, acceptance and to be able to experience the group as sustaining rather than persecutory. There is light from his hand which is holding rays very similar to those of the cocoon, which perhaps signals some creativity or potential route towards making relationships – he is no longer an isolate but can be one of a crowd. At least in the image he can see the way out – as in the previous image he is not totally submerged but is looking outwards.

In this sense there is a progression, as the image now has a head and can think and see the way forward. However, as Kim mentions himself, the way can also be backwards. The capacity to see involves risks and danger which Kim is clearly in touch with. Gabrielle notices this with reference to Kim's glasses which can enable him to see more clearly. Kim perceives this as investing the image with properties he did not have. Here there is a divergence of ways of understanding the detail in the picture which is notable because both therapist and client used the same 'words' in their feeling response to the self-portrait – melancholic and vulnerable. The emotions are more clearly on the surface.

There is a sense within the process of this session that Kim is attempting to move away from the therapeutic space with his preoccupation with his living accommodation, which is a genuine concern but has resonance between therapist and client. The therapist responds with containment of his anxiety rather than interpretation. The therapist sensed that any interpretative comment would not have been a holding experience, but acknowledged his need to gain an anchor to continue to be able to explore his inner struggle. The need for this framework, while he struggles with his preoccupation about his accommodation, seems to be symbolised by the tunnel in his image. It has to be strong and tight to be able to hold all his difficulties together.

Kim was struggling with his own sense of lack of self-confidence but also some fantasy about the therapeutic space – was this the 'accommodation' in his mind? How does the accommodation match up to the accommodation that the therapeutic space provides? Was he worried that he would have to leave the therapy if he is successful in his studies? Aspects of differentiation of himself as an individual are evident with the growing realisation of separation from the therapist. This seems to be an inevitable process but brings up painful ambivalence. When he becomes an independent person he will be leaving the mother/therapist and the act of finding his accommodation is a concrete reminder of this. There are ways of seeing the image which express this. The tunnel has associations of being in the womb and entering the birth canal which, once embarked upon, is an inevitable process, there is no turning back. The baby knows where he has come from but has no idea where he is going nor what it will be like when he gets there. Birth is a process which can only be anticipated. The only certainty is that it will happen. The actual experience is only made sense of after the event but this helps us to understand Kim's experience at this time. Klein describes this in the following way:

> I have put forward the hypothesis that the newborn baby experiences, both in the process of birth and in the adjustment to the post-natal situation, anxiety of a persecutory nature. This can be explained by the fact that the young infant, without being able to grasp it intellectually, feels unconsciously every discomfort as though it were inflicted on him by hostile forces. If comfort is given to him soon – in particular warmth, the loving way he is held, and the gratification of being fed – this gives rise to happier emotions. Such comfort is felt to come from good forces and, I believe, makes possible the infant's first loving relation to a person or, as the psycho-analyst would put it, to an object.
>
> (Klein 1959: 4)

It feels as if this is the stage which the therapy has reached. Kim is beginning his journey of separation from the mother/therapist.

The self-portrait symbolically represents a shift further along this road in an exploration of his identity – who is he? As Kim explains, it marks a moment again in which he feels there is no turning back. He is about to embark on his studies and the rest of his life. It is as if he has been born. He now exists separately in the world. What does he look like and how should he be if he is to be accepted into his group? – a problem that has always existed for him. As a mother would with a newborn infant, the therapist holds this anxiety but does not explore this in depth at this stage, realising how sensitive is the issue and the degree of difficulty that Kim is experiencing in bringing it into the session. Again the image provides a concrete 'container' to enable Kim to think about how to explore many different aspects of self, both internal and external. That is, he can explore how he looks but also how he feels and what is the experience of articulating from the inside what the outside is like. The portrait allows the process for his own self-analysis in the interaction between what is happening inside him and how that looks and is reflected on the outside. Kim describes how important this process has been to him and we note how this is different from the objective view of his tutors at interview.

There is a real sense that the process over time has enabled Kim to describe his 'image' to the therapist. Here in this session there is a clear picture of Kim's internal struggle for identity which is now openly explored with the therapist, since it feels as though he is now separate enough from her to do this. It is as if he is now already at a toddler stage: he is tentative, intrigued, feels obliged to join the group, but the world outside is frightening and if he wants to go back to 'mother' he needs to know she is there. One is reminded of the mother encouraging her child to join the group which begins the possibility of other relationships so that he no longer relies only on the therapist/mother to sustain him.

The emergence of his illness at this stage is noticeable, as this endorses the need for caring and to be looked after. It is interesting that the onset of his illness occurred during his late adolescence at the moment of leaving home and mother. Parallels can be drawn here in terms of the stage of the relationship with the therapist as dependency issues are struggled with. His real internal 'mess' or 'disease' is uncovered as he emerges from the cocoon, armour, and searches for an inner sense of self. To look inside and discover all is not 'well' is indeed a frightening process. His fear of transparency is still a theme related to his body but somehow the self-portrait makes him real – he is not a robotic-like figure but a real person with an emerging identity.

Figure 10 Under the skin.

Chapter 10

Dreams

KIM'S ACCOUNT

Using dreams as inspiration for pictures came about as a result of college homework. Part of the course was dedicated to psychology and sociology, subjects related to graphics by how we perceive and interpret images both on a conscious and a subconscious level. I was glad to have this 'academic' work, it reminded me that I was not stupid and also of secondary school which I enjoyed so much.

Jung and his theory about dreams came up in the psychology class and the tutor gave an example of how dreams could be interpreted. She asked if any of us had dreams recently that they would like to tell the class so that we could have the opportunity to do some analysing.

Earlier that year in June I had had a nightmare and made a small sketch when I woke up. I had always meant to make a proper picture out of it and now I had an opportunity. I suggested to the tutor that because we were all interested in art that maybe we should 'illustrate' our dreams. The tutor thought this was a good idea and set it as homework. I was not very popular for putting this forward but I didn't care. I had thrown down the gauntlet and I wanted to prove myself. Up to this point in the course I had been trying to impress the tutors and class through my dedication and the obvious extra (all my spare time in fact) time that I spent on projects. Now was my chance to SHOCK them as well. My confidence was returning.

I had been having some very strange dreams that year and, although I noted their contents, I could not understand (at that time) what had prompted them or what the significance of them was. The dream I had been waiting to have the time to illustrate was more of a nightmare: I was sitting down with my back to a fence and crowded around me, hemming me in, were a group of faceless strangers (faceless because they were in shadow – I could not see their faces) and my field of vision took in only the area immediately in front of me. My legs were naked (I do not know if I had any other clothes on) and these people were removing the skin from my shins and feet with their bare hands, ripping and peeling it back with their fingers. I observed the process unflinching and not bothering or wanting to struggle and get away. I was filled with a morbid curiosity about what was going on, as if, like the crowd, I was also curious to see what lay underneath my skin. I felt no pain in my dream and there was no blood. I remember being surprised – I didn't realise my skin was so thick! I was also surprised by my own knowledge of anatomy (never having studied human biology); as the strangers dug deeper there were glimpses of white bone through the muscle.

It was almost with relish that I took this picture into the class a week later and the teacher took a great interest in it, probably because it was the only dream that had been illustrated in the whole class. Due to lack of pictures to discuss the teacher set about analysing mine with vigour and determination. This was worrying and my plan started to backfire on me – I did not expect the tutor to be so accurate with her analysis and this was giving a lot of 'myself' away to the class when I had been so careful to protect myself up till then.

The analysis started with a list of what the people in the class would be feeling if they were in that (my dream) situation and these were: isolated, detached, trapped, disgusted, out of control (of the situation), curious, vulnerable, frightened, insecure and accepting. Next they made a list of all the symbolism: legs – movement and support, fence – boundaries/ security but also being trapped, people – social pressure, skin – covering/ façade, hands – probing, crowd – hurdle/blockage, underneath – exposing.

Lastly was a list of familiar sayings: 'near to the bone', 'thick skinned', 'under my skin', 'skin deep', 'too close for comfort', being 'torn apart'.

She concluded that the scene represented 'an anxiety that someone was trying to expose me'. She also suggested that the lack of pain and 'curious detachment' meant that I was trying to help this person do this. The tutor of course wanted to know if this was correct and asked me to comment, but I could hardly admit it, could I? My immediate thought was that this dream related to my therapy at Lancaster Rd. I could not tell the class that I attended 'therapy', I would have lost face and the image I had been cultivating since starting college – one of being cool, calm and collected and always in control. No doubt the class thought I was keeping quiet to cause intrigue.

I was quite content with this picture and happy to take it to show Gabrielle. Apart from its meaning, it was a 'good' picture, it aroused emotions in the viewer, I thought it was art. I was also interested to hear Gabrielle's interpretation. We soon arrived at the conclusion that it did indeed relate to my therapy, how we had been digging through the layers to find my real self. Of particular interest was my acknowledgement of being a willing client, my willingness initially arising from my desperation and need for help. This therapy had been my last hope, and as the therapy progressed I was learning to cope with life and with relationships.

Gabrielle asked if I would like to put THIS picture on the wall. I made an excuse – would it be a bit too gruesome and not beneficial for other clients? The truth was that this picture was precious to me: not just because of the image but more because it marked another level in my ability to express myself in my pictures. I felt triumphant at managing to get a picture that was inside my head out onto paper where other people could see it. And yet I wanted to hold onto it. However, I also wanted to give back something to the centre, in appreciation of its existence, that I was able to find help there. My pride had a final say in the matter. I mean how many other clients would have TWO pictures on the wall to their credit?

THERAPIST'S ACCOUNT

Kim made this image after some time in therapy, although we did not discuss it until four months later. He had been accepted for college but was extremely anxious about it. At the time of having the dream, he was preoccupied with thoughts about whether he would be as good as the other students and would he be able to keep up. Most of all he was terrified of the contact with the other students and his communications to me were as if he was a 'leper'. He feared their disapproval, their rejection, their humiliation. He had ben living a hermit's life and he feared contact. He was more familiar with his isolation and depression.

The way Kim expressed his anxiety was in an obsessive preoccupation about his new accommodation. He also communicated his despair and described having recurrent suicidal thoughts. It was as if the door had been opened with the possibility of a chink of light. He was terrified, terrified of failure, terrified of success. He did not feel entitled to or worthy of anything more than his dreary unhappy life.

At this time he was extremely tense and in a high state of anxiety. I was still the only person he saw each week and I was aware of his enormous investment in the therapeutic relationship. With his lack of contact with the world outside, he was still very vulnerable. I needed to work supportively with his search for accommodation. I sensed the fragility of his inner world and he seemed to need help in thinking about how to face the problems, fears and anxieties which he perceived to belong to the outer world.

It was during this time that he had this dream but it was not until he was settled at college that it returned to this image form. It seemed that he made a deliberate choice to hold onto the dream until he was able to work with it. He needed to be more anchored to be able to share it with me.

Once he had started the course and found somewhere to live, he brought this image of his dream, which interestingly had been a subject that was part of his course. In the picture there were two figures peeling the skin away from a pair of legs that are suspended in the air. The wound is very deep and their hands are bloody. The skin had been gouged out to the bone. Behind are three unknown figures. I was struck with this image as it had been drawn with a freedom and intensity not expressed in his previous images. The marks express a genuineness and spontaneity not previously explored. Kim described the dream in the following way:

> It was dark, I was surrounded by people I didn't recognise, they made their way to me. I was backed against a wooden fence. I was surrounded by no way out. I wasn't panicking or thinking about trying to escape. I didn't know these people but I didn't feel afraid of them. The people at the front started peeling the skin from my legs, by sinking their fingers in and pulling it back. It peeled off very easily like soft clay and I was amazed at the lack of blood. I felt no pain as I watched intently eager to see what was underneath. I saw the thickness of my skin and glimpses of bone through the layers of muscle. I sat abstractedly and watched with perverse fascination and disgust at my anatomy being exposed.

He spoke with excitement as though he was reaching another level in himself and, through a greater depth of spontaneity, was able to make contact with something real.

Although Kim talked about a perverse fascination and disgust at his anatomy being exposed he also described the lack of pain and a detachment from the experience. I reflected to Kim that his reaction to the dream perhaps mirrored feelings he had about himself. He talked about the fact that he was full of self-loathing, contempt; he was concerned that his behaviour was perverse, and he also felt as if he was an observer of life and his own behaviour. I felt at the time that what was most significant was how he described the lack of pain and my sense of this was that he was not yet connected to it. He said his tutor had made some suggestions to him that someone might have been trying to expose him near to the bone. The lack of pain and curious detachment suggested that 'he', the person in the dream, was allowing or perhaps even helping the person to do this.

This way of understanding it helped him make the link between this picture and the start of therapy and his fears about what might happen to him. This made me think about the time when Kim started therapy and had feared humiliation. He feared that, if he exposed himself, I might observe him as if he was a scientific experiment. He had felt a need for his defences to be securely intact in case I was to cause him ridicule. He was however able to let down these protective masks, peel back the skin and bear the pain. Perhaps the pain was more bearable than the overwhelming experience of emptiness that he had felt before.

I reflected to him that, although, on first impression, I felt the image to be bloody and messy. The image, however, I felt paralleled our developing relationship in therapy. I sensed that Kim was 'unpeeling his skins' in therapy, which he showed by his dream and picture. I said that there felt to be a passion in both his picture and in his commitment to change, and it was at this point that he expressed the anxiety that he feared a move to art college would end the therapeutic relationship and that the sessions would have to come to an end.

In the dream Kim seemed to think that the legs in the air were his. The skin is being torn away by two other people which suggests a passivity, the idea of things being done to him by other people. In the early days of our relationship he was eager to place his trust in me, and for me to provide a container for his fears and anxieties and provide a cocoon for his metamorphosis. But there are two people doing things to him – I suggested to him that maybe one of them was him moving into the role of helping in the work which, although bloody, might indicate that he was taking some control over his life. He thought about this and seemed to absorb it.

OVERVIEW

This is powerful material for us to grapple with. Visually, the image is extremely graphic. At the time, the therapist was waiting and listening to the profound nature of these communications which is the most important feature of the work. The complexity of the symbolism in this dream will take some time to understand fully and even after the end of therapy fresh meanings, insights and connections may emerge. The dream represents a rawness, with genuine statements from the unconscious, and the image is striking in this respect. Working at this greater intensity and depth there might be some anxiety on the part of the therapist that she would not understand it all and that something might be 'missed', but it is not possible to make a full interpretation of dreams nor indeed is it necessarily desirable.

As Kim's experience of his tutorial bears out, he trusted the group with his deep self-revelation in the belief that he would be praised and this caught him off guard. Instead, one gets the feeling that he was bombarded and overwhelmed by other people's interpretations and words assigning meaning to the image he had brought to the group. This seemed to be more about their own need for meaning rather than understanding Kim's associations to his dream. What is interesting is that, although Kim seemed to enjoy the sense of occasion at first, it quickly turned into a nightmare similar to the dream itself. The group 'attacked' his image in their urgency to make sense of it, seizing upon it and almost ripping it (and Kim) apart. Such is the powerful nature of this image, the group response was in fact an enactment of what is happening in the picture.

We can see how this was not at all helpful for Kim in coming to his own understanding of what it meant for him, which is what he then brought to the session with Gabrielle. This is a clear example of the way that interpretations can be misinterpretations which tend to stay on the surface and do not have any resonance or significance for the person concerned. Kim was not ready to take in many of these comments from the tutorial, and they merely added to his confusion as he was not in the right place in which he could make sense of them. Fortunately, he had his therapy session to go to for that. But, as was discussed in the introduction, premature interpretation can be destructive and damaging and is more often than not due to the therapist's own need for understanding and answers more than the client's. As art therapists we have to be sensitive to the clumsiness and inappropriateness of casual interpretation or chance remark – naming an image in words can cause great distress and anxiety when the client may be struggling to depict something entirely different. This was clearly demonstrated in the tutorial. Any important material will re-emerge in subsequent sessions and remaining in a state of 'not knowing' is crucial in the interaction between therapist and client to allow the understanding and symbolism of images and material to emerge in their own time.

One is reminded of the importance of Bion's work in helping us as therapists to 'live in the question' and not close down possibilities of meaning. This is demonstrated by Gabrielle's capacity to hold on to her thoughts and yet keep possibilities of meaning in her mind, waiting for Kim to make sense of his image. It doesn't appear that he comes for answers, but the image raised genuine concerns that deeply preoccupy him. The graphic nature of the image evokes a strong response from the viewer as one is moved by its impact. Kim actively set out to do this – to shock people with his image – but this is also testament to his shocking experience. Looking at images like this promotes an aesthetic response which causes a move from passivity to activity, which was Kim's intention. When the image is gruesome or repulsive, the viewer may feel disgust or want to turn away. To cope with the difficult feelings that might be generated one 'action' might be to then block off the affect of the image and ascribe meaning to it, which is our understanding of the response in the tutorial class. Case and Dalley (1992) provide us with a detailed discussion of the importance of the aesthetic response in art therapy, but, for our purposes here, it is noticeable how the therapist used her response to the image and the aesthetic feeling states that are aroused in the counter-transference. She is aware of the powerful nature of this process and is therefore skilled in remaining open and available to all the different aspects of meaning in the picture. Gabrielle worked with Kim's interpretation and did not impose her views, but kept her thoughts held in mind, reflecting them back to him at the appropriate moment so that he might make sense of them.

In this first dream (Figure 10, 'Under the skin'), we see someone tearing at the flesh on the leg and there is a sense of dissociation from the pain which might be Kim's way of dealing with it. He can see pain but does not feel it; he could see no blood but the image is 'bloody'; there is a feeling of savagery, attack and a vulture-like experience, tearing at flesh to expose the bone which is not taken up in the discussion. There are elements of both pleasure and pain in this image in that some pleasure might have been aroused by watching objectively such a painful experience. He articulates this experience, but also one wonders whether this was how Kim experienced the therapist watching him. There is a sense that Gabrielle might be active in the process of helping him but perhaps hurting him at the same time.

This is a fascinating example of the way the image can embody the feeling which provides the vehicle or means through which Kim can acknowledge feelings for himself. As we have discussed, Schaverien (1992) describes in detail how the embodied image can take on the feelings of the client and this holds them safely until the client is ready to incorporate them for himself. Embodied in this dream image seem to be questions about who these other people are – are they Gabrielle and his tutor? Is he trying to find a new therapist in his tutor? Is he furious with Gabrielle in his anxiety that perhaps the sessions might end, and, by anticipating feelings of loss, defending against his angry feelings? This anger was beginning to surface in the last session and this is how he is beginning to express it – feeling torn apart. But in his surfacing anger, he might fear he will damage her or fear her response. Either way, this powerful image may unconsciously provide a means to maintain the link with the therapist and in this way keep her interested and engaged.

The image of the dream contains most of these feelings and they remain in the session in this form until some understanding takes place, when Kim is able to articulate his anxieties about leaving verbally. He also comes to understand that he is an observer of his own inner pain, as he understands Gabrielle to be as well. Is this dream symbolic of him tearing off his outer layers, his mask, his cocoon, which has masked his real self for so long? It is a dramatic way to experience this and discover what really is inside.

It felt useful and containing for him that Gabrielle could see the blood and experience the sense of exposure and tolerate the degree of mess and horror that he is beginning to express. Bion (1977) describes how the traumatised person experiences 'pain but not the suffering'. He is in the pain, overwhelmed by it, but the pain is not in him. The image seems to provide a means through which this pain can become incorporated into himself and thereby he can tolerate it rather than being overwhelmed by it. In this way he does not have to remain detached from it. Tracey (1991) suggests that a solid container, the therapist and also in this case the image, allows the pain to be lived with, suffered not denied.

Figure 11 Barrier.

DREAM – 'BARRIER'

Most of the pictures I had been doing for my therapy were usually executed in one evening, a maximum of three hours spent on them. This was a time limit I set myself to ensure it did not interfere with my college work. The next dream picture was the product of several evenings work, a luxury I could afford due to the Easter holidays. This picture also benefited from the short period of time between the dream and the picture. I had been able literally to 'freeze frame' the image in my head and get it down onto paper like a 'still' from a movie. I use the word film because this dream was like being in a movie, a science fiction movie. . . .

The first part I remember is walking up to an alien spacecraft. People were entering the spaceship under their own free will (or so it appeared) as if the aliens were inviting us to have a look at their advanced technology. The entrance to the ship was full of white light so that as people entered they became silhouettes and I was following close behind a friend (I cannot remember who) when an alarm sounded and red lights flashed in the glass canopy above my head. I heard a voice warning me: 'You are too close to the person in front – you must enter alone.' I believed that this was projected into my head and that no one else could hear it; this made me suspicious. Why should I alone hear this message? Did THEY have an ulterior motive?

I decided to go back and turned around; this caused even more alarm, they obviously did not want me to leave so I started running and so did a couple of people who were behind me. Two aliens (who looked very much like humans) were erecting a fence around the ship. I was right, it was a trap. The fence was not very high and made of a thick metallic hose (one and a half to two inches in diamater) loosely slung between posts. I thought I would be able to dive over or under it but when I got close the hose swung about to meet me and, where it made contact with my arms which I brought up to protect myself, it left raised red marks like burns or acid. I guessed it was some kind of electric fence and I persevered in trying to cross it somehow but only managed to burn both my forearms very badly. Unlike in my other dream, these wounds were very painful.

The couple who had run were caught at the electric fence by the aliens but I had to escape. I looked right up the line of the fence and saw the fence had not been completed so I ran up to this break pursued by the two aliens on the other side. I managed to get to the breach before they did. I was free, or so I thought.

I went home. Home was a sort of communal living area in run-down and squalid slums. To my horror my flatmates were complacent about the aliens' takeover – I realised that this was because they had already been, or were willing to be, taken over. I wanted desperately to find someone like me so that I wouldn't be on my own, and I wasn't feeling too good. I was becoming ill, feeling weak and fatigued, sick in the stomach, my head ached and so did my limbs. It felt like I was dying and I put that down to the lack of medical attention for the injuries I sustained at the alien electric fence. I was becoming seriously depressed as my situation appeared more and more helpless. There seemed to be the odd person who could still feel pity for me (my deteriorating condition). I remember a girl from college being one.

I felt like giving up, there was nowhere safe for me to go. People who used to know me didn't tell the aliens where I was but neither did they help me. And still the aliens pursued me in a dogged relentless manner, just waiting for me to give up. Eventually I could go on no further and entered the ruins of another slum. I was trying to hide under the table in a dark kitchen when they finally found me, their figures loomed in silhouette against the light through the outside door. They offered to treat my wounds, saying 'we can make you better if you join us'. What they wanted me to do was to give in – stop resisting. One of them had a large syringe in his hands and I remember another girl from class being one of them. I don't remember what she was doing, but I knew that she didn't care about me. I turned their offer down and they left. My wounds aggravated me and I was seriously ill now. I was going to die in that dirty, rotten, smelly place. My last thoughts were that I was on my own, I could not trust anyone because there were no humans left.

When I had made notes on my dream I selected the three 'frames' which I thought could be illustrated as a triptych. I wanted to try and tell the whole story. I never got around to doing the other pictures. I selected this frame because it had some action in it as well as some horror. It was very important to convey the gesture of the hands/arms up in defence. To do this I actually put my own hands up in front of my face; the problem of drawing the right hand was that, being right handed, I had to use my left hand and drawing caused me some physical discomfort (and pain even several days afterwards). The 'hose' is collaged to give it a three-dimensional feel, so is the mound on the thumb on the right hand. The burns on the arms are actually burnt with the flame from a candle and the blood was varnished to give it a wet appearance. One other aspect of its realism is that it is life-size.

I started to analyse this dream picture myself. Firstly I considered if there had been any recent experiences which my subconscious had filtered in the way that 'rubbish' often finds its way into dreams. *Invasion of the Body Snatchers* had been on the television just a couple of days before. An older memory would have been the illness when I was nineteen and the feelings of hopelessness and alienation could be more recently associated with my depression. I felt these things needed to be recognised to put the dream into context.

I believed this dream reflected my feelings and fears about my depression, my loss of identity and subsequent therapy. When I was severely depressed I felt as if I was an alien living on this planet. I did not understand what motivated people, how their lives seemed solely to revolve around earning money and socialising. In my dream the situation was reversed – I was the only human and everybody else was alien! In either case I was the odd one out. There was a point in my therapy when I realised that I was getting better and that frightened me. I had found a sort of security in my depression and it had become a core for my identity.

If I was totally cured that part of my identity would be lost. I had become obsessed with the idea of the suffering melancholic artist, and I clung to it. It was also an excuse I could use for my failures, for not being able to cope and not being able to relate to other people. At this point I was not sure whether I really did want to be cured.

That was as far as I could take the analysis of myself but Gabrielle was able to see much more in it. Her first comment was that the electric fence represented the barrier that I had put up myself to avoid interacting with the world and the people in it. I considered the care that I had taken in illustrating the barrier and thought she could be right, not only that but the way that cutting myself off from the world was damaging, like the electric fence. Gabrielle asked me what was I trying to escape to? In my dream I was trying to go 'back' and that was symbolised by ruins and slums, a bleak and barren landscape that was not at all inviting yet I sought security there. These 'ruins' were the ruins of my past, the result of the way I had been living my life wrong. She recognised my struggle between wanting to go back to what was familiar and the part of me that wanted to change (though I had known all along but not wanted to admit it that there was no point in going back, there was nothing to go back to). This helped me finally to turn my back on the past and start to look forward. Initially I had to blinker myself because there is always the temptation to look back and brood but this is a waste of mental energy. It is better to visualise a positive future and try to make plans that might make it come about. Gabrielle suggested that this picture should go up on the wall, saying that she felt that it might help my barrier to come down. This felt like a challenge in her suggestion that I had a great deal invested in having my protective coil in place. That may well have been true, but I still didn't feel ready to change.

THERAPIST'S ACCOUNT

The second dream Kim brought a few months later. It seemed his time at college was bringing his unconscious thoughts to the surface and he felt a need to think about these in the sessions. It sounded as though his anxiety about his competence had proved to be unfounded as he had succeeded in submitting a number of projects which were highly accredited. During the first term he had worked long, intense hours often into the early hours of the morning. While this was reflected in the quality of the work, he felt it also acted as a smoke screen against having to deal with his relationships with fellow students. It allowed him to remain emotionally cocooned from the pleasure, frustration and disappointment of real relationships. We spent a lot of time examining this, as underneath he still feared their rejection, feared that he was empty and had nothing to offer. He didn't believe that they would want to spend time with him.

This dream took place away from college while he was staying with his parents for the weekend. As he told me about the dream he was sombre and troubled by it. His account was the following: He said he was entering an alien spaceship being followed closely behind by a friend. An alarm sounded and lights flashed telling him he had to go ahead alone. This made him feel suspicious, so he turned around to go back. He started to run in an attempt to get away, in his path were two aliens who looked like human beings erecting an electric fence of thick hose. He tried to dive under or over but it kept swinging around, and when it contacted his right arm, it left red marks like acid burns, which were very painful. He said he felt driven to escape and saw that one of the ends of the fence had not been finished, and so he managed to cross the line of this fence and squeeze through.

In the next part of the dream, Kim described how he went back to his communal living space which was run down and squalid. In the dream his other flatmates seemed complacent about the takeover by the aliens. He described desperately trying to find someone like him so he did not feel so alone. He felt at this moment fatigued, sick in the stomach, his head and limbs ached. He thought he was dying, which he understood to be due to lack of medical treatment but he got only pity from the people around him. He felt like giving up, feeling unprotected, with nowhere safe to go. He felt he would never have anyone to trust as, when he talked about this with the people in his dream, he got no reaction because they were no longer human.

The dream had been very painful for Kim. It seemed to be about his sense of alienation from his peer group at college. All the other students were much younger with a very different life experience. He described how he had devoted a lot of his time to painting and remaining solitary and isolated – the dream seemed to reflect this sense of isolation but also a sense of being trapped. We discussed how this aspect seemed to be associated with staying with his parents again which brought back all the feelings of being emotionally trapped and alienated from his family but also the memories of his illness. He described his thoughts, during the time of his illness, ulcerative colitis, of death and experience of a profound sense of isolation. He had pushed his friends away then as he had felt they would reject him because of his imperfections. These anxieties seem to be resurfacing in the dream and particularly seem to be connected to his deep fear of the surgical treatment which he narrowly escaped. The removal of a part of the large intestine, a full colostomy was not necessary, but the terror of this possibility still seemed to be around. The hands in the dream, which are in the foreground of the image, have been burnt by a thick metal coil behind them. He described the burn like an 'acid burn, corrosive, sharp and very painful'. I wondered to myself whose hands were they? Were they mine, his mother's, the possible surgeon's? Did he fear my hands could burn him?

Kim was in a sombre mood when he talked about this image and I was struck by the fact that he did not seem overwhelmed or very distressed.

His mood seemed less turbulent than the image. When I pointed this out, Kim told me he had very quickly written down the dream on waking and then shortly afterwards made this powerful picture. This seems to have acted as an effective vehicle of containment and he was able to process this in such a way that he could communicate the experience clearly. Some of the destructive feelings were no longer festering away on the inside, but he felt more in control of them as he put them down on paper in the knowledge that he could bring them to the session.

I talked with Kim about this and thought with him about the people in the dream. He felt that they were no longer human which seemed to heighten his sense of isolation. The image is full of intensity and I was struck with the sense of his inside being placed outside both in the dream and in the picture, but as yet he could only risk expressing the full range of emotional experiences in this medium. His emotional fears of being left isolated, out of contact with his fellow humans, were being expressed. In the picture we see a burnt-out city in the background which portrays a sense of desolation and emptiness. It had been bombed, an empty shell with no inner core, and I felt this linked with the feelings he experienced when he was seriously ill. His body felt bombed and it was as if his inner world felt bombed and burnt out. I was reminded of the previous dream in which the hands seem to be tearing at his body to get at the inside. Perhaps the dreams are sequential in the respect that in the first there was no connection to the pain but, once inside, the pain is acute and intense. It is painful to expose your feelings and inner self and this seems to be recognised by Kim as the pain could now be located on to the 'metal coil', symbolic of his insides which needed treatment, intervention and healing.

At the time I was left not fully understanding the correlation with Kim's experience of colitis and of feeling burnt out, although there were links between the metal coil and his intestine that he felt was destroying his life. The dream was distressing but it was not frightening and I don't think Kim was frightened by it as we struggled to make sense of it together. I was also experiencing some changes in Kim in terms of his ability to be open as to what he shared of himself, becoming less frightened of the world outside, and he was beginning to make some tentative relationships. He seemed to be less fearful of being rejected and I had the feeling that more of his true self was emerging, with less reliance on his 'false' persona. His emotional life was being expressed on paper, if not fully in his life outside. It felt as though he was becoming a more three-dimensional person with authentic contact in our relationship.

We talked about this and reflected on the fact that this three-dimensional aspect was also present in the image in that there was a foreground and a background. This identified for him that he was a person with an inside with feelings and thoughts that could be shared and explored. There was a space in there that was not entirely empty and paradoxically the picture which seemed to be about a dead city seemed to show that he was more alive and able to feel pain. This seemed to mirror Kim's struggle as to whether he was to be overwhelmed by the dead and empty feelings of the past or be anchored by his capacity to look inside, be reflective and develop his creativity. It is the creative act itself which involves intense and constant self-analysis in the interplay between inside and outside processes. I felt this struggle was personified in the hands that were being 'bloodied' and burnt by the coil behind them. The coil represented illness, destruction and possible disintegration, the dismembered part of him. The hands, beautifully drawn, represent both the possibility of destruction and the potential for creativity and health which can be seen in both the doctor's and the artist's hands. It is with his hands that he will be able to create as a designer, and also to make these pictures to make sense of his conflicting emotions and turmoil and put together some feeling of control over his life. It was the artist part of him that could hold these different parts of himself together. The bleak and desolate aspects were balanced with a creative response to pain. Within the therapeutic boundaries of our relationship, Kim was developing a profound sense of himself as a creator and the realisation that his hands have the potential for both self-destruction and creativity. I suggested Kim might want to put the picture on the wall. My thinking at the time was that his savage and aggressive feelings might diminish if they were in a public arena, which might be likened to sharing some similar material in a group. He had taken the risk of sharing these intense feelings with me, which I felt was a shift for him, and I wanted to acknowledge that in some way and help him think about how important were these aspects of himself. I felt I wanted to let him see that it was acceptable to be angry and openly express this.

OVERVIEW

After sharing one dream and coming to some degree of understanding, this led the way to the next one which again features hands as both destructive and creative objects. The second dream has more instant quality to the image as compared to the first which he needed to hold onto until he felt safe enough to process it. Kim's description of the way he made the image was most interesting, with a three-dimensional collage in the actual 'burning' with a candle to portray the burn, the varnish as the blood and the use of the left hand posing problems of control, unpredictability and uncoordination. Actual loss of control in the execution of the picture lays him open to accident and risk and the resultant possible loss of perfection. The feelings are enacted in the making of the image – in the dream he is burnt, out of control; the hands are used for self-defence, he is wanting to trust his own judgement and intuition to escape: a fascinating process which makes it come alive. As Kim points out, it is even life-size.

Here we can see the fundamental importance of allowing this voice to be heard and Kim even begins to analyse the dream himself before bringing it to Gabrielle. No longer does he feel the need for others to do this for him (tear him apart), but he can now begin to think about possibilities for himself. Kim talks about the *Invasion of the Body Snatchers*, makes links with his illness and his experience of feeling 'the only one', as he begins to explore his own associations to the material. It may be an indication of the degree of isolation he is experiencing in that he is the 'only human', but this self-reliance marks a real shift in the confidence in himself. Here we can see the outcome of waiting by the therapist with the interpretation so that he can find the answers himself. Once again this is endorsed by Winnicott's view:

> It is very important when the client is regressed to earliest infancy that the analyst shall not know the answer except in so far as the client gives the clues. Magical interpretations pre-empt the client's separateness, he is robbed of a mind of his own. The mother does not give the infant a feed, the infant gives the mother the opportunity to feed him. The clues provided by the client facilitate the analyst's capacity to interpret. It is not so much a question of giving the baby satisfaction as of letting the baby find and come to terms with the object.
>
> (Winnicott 1965: 59–69)

The dreams also seem to suggest a shift from isolation to greater integration in his relationships. The first image is blurred and bloody, the second appears more clear and clinical. The first is a solitary but passive experience with people doing violent things to him, the second involves activity, movement and interaction with other people, both human and non-human. The friend he travels with and has to leave may represent the therapist and the dream seems to depict what he fears he will experience without her. He is deeply suspicious of other people and how they will relate to him and fears they will hurt him and get inside him.

The real fear of intrusion is raised by the syringe and the prospect of incision, but interestingly this sets up the idea that there is something inside to cut into. Inside and outside are represented by the actual three-dimensional properties of the image. There is both foreground and background in the picture and so it has depth, but also in his symbolism of travel and going places in the dream there is movement, which perhaps reflects inner shifts within Kim. There is a dynamic process as he wrestles with the coil and attempts to escape. It is possible he has found his way out of the tunnel, as in Figure 8. There is a space inside which is becoming less frightened of bad feelings and he is fully in touch with the pain. It feels as if Kim now has a greater tolerance of ambivalent feelings, he can take in bad feelings and hold on to them within himself. He also comes to realise that he cannot go back to the previous pain, the slums of his existence, which he finds potentially comforting but he knows will not be helpful. This relates to the cocoon and Cornwell's ideas of returning to past defence strategies for survival. Kim has moved on from that, as is now made conscious.

If we look further at the material of the dream, if the friend he is travelling with is Gabrielle, the two aliens might also be her and his tutor. They continue to pursue him and these 'two aliens' also have associations with the problem of the couple and the clash of loyalties between his parents that he experienced in his childhood. The other people that are not 'human' lead him to differentiate people with feelings and his reliance on the therapist in his need to be recognised, be responded to and taken seriously (Kohut and Wolff 1978). Although Gabrielle is not actually represented in the image, she is in the dream and to some extent he is relating to all these aspects of her in the transference. Bringing dreams to the session at this stage in the therapy is noted by Gabrielle. His anxiety about ending has enabled him to bring deeper material to the sessions and the more contained environment provides him with the possibility of allowing more unconscious material to surface. The ending of the sessions, the death of the therapy seems to link with fear of his own death in the dream. This brings to the surface one of his most terrifying fears – annihilation. His fragile ego is struggling to survive and could so easily be wiped out. He is soft and vulnerable as if he is now out of his shell.

The use of the diary appears to be crucial in providing him with another strategy for survival. Kim has now learnt to put immediate thoughts and images in writing, which holds them in his mind until there is time to make an image of them and then take them to therapy to explore them in depth. However, he was only able to bring them when he had found accommodation and felt safe enough to be able to look inside himself again. Also, as Kim describes, his accommodation is 'very nice indeed' – not the slums that he dreaded which are represented in the dream.

There is another important aspect to be considered here. Kim is now committed to regular creative activity as a requirement for his studies. Indeed he states how his college work is taking over his time and his space for therapy work is limited and has to be 'fitted in'. If we look at the processes involved in creative activity, it is clear that this demands introspection, reflection and personal evaluation. Much of the literature on this subject discusses the intensity of this process and how much of the image-making process involves an interplay between the unconscious and conscious. Creativity involves chaos, uncertainty and vulnerability as well as the stages of feeling that something has worked and been made successfully. In his description of creative activity, Ehrenzweig (1967) shows us clearly the importance of these processes in the 'deceptive chaos of art's vast substructure', deceptive because there is a 'hidden order in this chaos', the hidden order of the unconscious. 'Something like a true conversation takes place between an artist and his own work' (Ehrenzweig 1967: 57).

It might be useful to expand this a little further, as Ehrenzweig's ideas greatly inform our thinking and certainly speak to us about the intensity of Kim's experience. He describes how the interaction between the artist, the idea and medium allows contact with the unconscious.

> The medium by frustrating the artist's purely conscious intentions allows him to contact more submerged parts of his personality and draw them up for conscious contemplation. While the artist struggles with his medium, unknown to himself he wrestles with his unconscious personality revealed by the work of art. Taking back from the work on a conscious level what has been projected into it on an unconscious level is perhaps the most fruitful and painful result of creativity.
>
> (Ehrenzweig 1967: 57)

During the artistic process there is a time of 'unconscious scanning' where integration of the work, the picture and the artist's personality takes place. 'This total integration can only be controlled by the empty state of unconscious scanning which alone is capable of overcoming the fragmentation in art's surface structure' (Ehrenzweig 1967: 30).

We can see how, by bringing his dreams in picture form, Kim has been able to make full use of this process. It is for this reason that the art therapist must be someone who has personally experienced these creative processes in depth to be able to understand their significance for the client. Over time Kim's images express greater depths of his unconscious and the artist in the art therapist has been available to these communications through understanding the processes involved. The images provided the vehicle for the expression of his dream experience and are imbued with real fear of illness and death. This marks a shift in his capacity to express this deeper anxiety.

In this sense, Gabrielle has double the amount of material to work with – the account of the dreams and the images which portray them, which are a condensed version of his experience. Kim aptly described this, in the portrayal of the second dream, as a freeze frame of a film, an uncompleted triptych. What is interesting for us to note is that he felt the picture of the first dream was not suitable for display, as this image represented another level of consciousness which he was not ready to show and was able to acknowledge that this might be disturbing for others. His real self is now showing in his pictures, not the mask that he was presenting before. His need to retain it was an important indication that it was precious and held great significance for him. Here there is a different emphasis in the way he is working through his feelings in the images. There is a rawness to them, his feelings are on the surface. Gabrielle's suggestion of putting the second image on the wall she likens to sharing his deep feelings with a group and thus being a concrete way of actually working through this difficulty of joining the group. Having recognised this, he could see how it would help him focus on this particular problem as he has already experienced it and can also visualise it from the dream. The picture symbolically represents his dream experience and therefore holds the meaning over time for Kim to make full use of it in his attempts to work it through.

For Kim, by learning to be able to use his art work in this way, he is beginning to trust himself and his emotions and is becoming a person in his ability to look inside. The shifts and changes are becoming more noticeable, there is uncertainty and a capacity for ambivalence. This allows new issues to emerge. As the process develops and the understanding of the images emerges, Kim is able to articulate his anxiety about the end of the sessions verbally. This was already surfacing in the previous session and the therapist was able to wait until Kim could speak of it for himself. There is also a sense that he fears being exposed, possibly again relating to his illness, the fear of which becomes fully conscious in this dream. He re-experiences the reality of his fear and preoccupation and Gabrielle responds by making reference to the hands possibly being those of a surgeon and fears of intrusive painful incision which may relate to her own anxiety about being intrusive, a 'non-human' or an alien. The relationship between therapist and client is coming more fully into view. One is reminded of Freud's suggestion that the analyst model himself on the surgeon by putting aside his human sympathy and adopting an attitude of emotional coldness. Maybe somewhere in Kim's mind this may be a reference to his previous therapist whom he did experience as cold and clinical. It could also be a reference to his feelings about Gabrielle and the 'intrusive' part of her that they have been working with throughout their interactions. What is of interest to us here is thoughts about Kim's experience of the therapist. The dreams seem to incorporate fears and fantasies in relation to this. Who is she? What is she really like? The therapist is becoming more of a person in Kim's mind, and perhaps there is some connection in the material with his previous experience in therapy. In their article entitled the 'Persecutory therapist', Meares and Hobson (1977) outline six main features of therapy resulting in feelings of persecution, one of which is 'opaqueness of the therapy' and another is 'intrusion'. It seems helpful to describe each of these in turn.

> 'Intrusion can occur in another way which is very different from interrogation. A highly intuitive therapist is in danger of making accurate understanding statements too early. Then, at best, the client is afraid and avoids further exposure; at worst, he or she feels invaded and attacked inside by the 'magical' therapist who can control the hidden self which, now, is no longer his 'own'. He can surrender his autonomy and sense of identity in a prolonged dependence upon the 'all knowing' therapist. Such disasters can occur in response to purely non-verbal communications by a 'too-understanding therapist'.
>
> (Meares and Hobson 1977: 30)

They continue:

> The avoidance of intrusion calls for a balance of intimacy and distance with a continuing respect for the client's personal, private space. It involves what one of the authors terms a rhythm of 'aloneness – togetherness'. Aloneness is distinguished from isolation, alienation or loneliness; and togetherness is differentiated from a fantasy of fusion and blissful union (Hobson 1974).
>
> (Meares and Hobson 1977: 350)

In contrast the opaque therapist is described thus:

> He impedes the client 's movement towards a healthy reduction of his distorted perception of others, by failing to allow him to make this comparison between what is 'illusion' and what is 'actual'. Unless at the appropriate time – and this timing is crucial – the therapist reveals what he is like, the client has no opportunity to test out fantasy against fact. He is hindered in his efforts to discover his identity. Since all is illusion he can come to believe that all is distortion – his experience of himself and his perception of other people. Then all his emotional responses are 'neurotic' there is no healthy bit left.
>
> (Meares and Hobson 1977: 353)

These accounts are helpful to us not only in terms of the dream material but also in understanding Kim's overall therapy experience. His experience of the therapeutic relationship that has developed with Garbielle is central to his capacity to communicate and thus facilitate his own recovery. The central dynamic between them has been fear of invasion and intrusion and this has been worked through. He is beginning to differentiate the therapist in his mind and can also tolerate angry, negative feelings towards her. This is of paramount importance in this process and as we can see by the process over time and what Kim has brought in his dreams, the idealisation has shifted to let in the previously denied 'bad' feelings which can now be tolerated. We have listened to the client 's experience and learned from it (Casement 1987). The images and dreams are rich and draw us fully into Kim's imaginative and deeper inner world. Perhaps it is safer for him to bring his dreams when he is not feeling so dependent on the therapist and his ego is stronger. There is not such a risk of swamping or being swamped and equally we see how the therapist is not repulsed by the images or overwhelmed by the material and does not react adversely against them in her counter-transference. She is seen to be able to take in difficult feelings, which provides a good model for Kim in struggling to make sense of his own feelings and concerns. He comes to understand that the destructive and creative hands are needed for his 'self-defence' as no one else will do it for him. Good and bad can be tolerated together. As the dependency is worked through, he realises that he is essentially alone in the world.

Figure 12 Gabrielle.

Chapter 11

Relationship with the therapist

KIM'S ACCOUNT

Little progress was made with the first (male) therapist. This was more my fault than anybody else's. I had started playing a game with him, to see if he was as clever as he thought he was. He wasn't going to catch me out or trip me up with his questions – I could not be defined so easily. He didn't understand that I was unique in my suffering! This had not instilled much faith in me and I wondered whether I could be helped by any kind of psychotherapy at all. However, I did feel more at ease in Gabrielle's company.

Generally speaking I had always found it easier to talk to girls/women. I had more female friends than male but then I had few male friends anyway. In the days when I would go out I enjoyed women's company because I felt I had more in common with them than with men. Then again, maybe these were relationships of convenience because being with women meant that I could dress how I wanted to and wear make-up – things I could not have done in the company of men. Women seem to find 'pretty men' more acceptable.

I didn't feel as if Gabrielle was trying to trick me into saying something that would make it easy for her to label me. The questions she asked did not sound as if they would be used to pigeon-hole me. Gabrielle seemed genuinely concerned about my predicament and sincere in wanting to help me. I felt relieved at being treated like a person and not just a client. Up until this point the only person I had told how sad I was and that I wanted to end it all was the girlfriend of a friend of mine. She was so concerned about my mental state that she made me promise to her that I would seek medical help and phone her every day in the meantime. While I was talking to her about the way I felt I was overcome by grief and sadness and started crying – I didn't really want to kill myself, and yet what was the point of living when there is nothing to look forward to or to make you happy. I had kept these feelings so well hidden that when she told her boyfriend of our conversation he found it hard to believe because he thought I was OK. Not only would I not have got upset if I had told him, I would probably not have told the him in the first place. I could not tell my male friends the truth about my situation – too much pride to lose and my ego was at stake I guess.

It was easier for me to tell the truth to Gabrielle because she was a woman and therefore I was not worried about being judged as a man. Because she did not know me from before she would not have seen my achievements or how the mighty had fallen. Another reason I found it easier to talk to Gabrielle rather than to friends was because I did not feel guilty about it and did not feel she would be overwhelmed by my burden. Depression is infectious and I didn't want to get people down. Rather than never having any good news for them I would give them no news at all – I stopped seeing them. But I didn't feel guilty unburdening my problems to Gabrielle because it was her job. In a way it was a sort of purging process because, after telling another person about the reasons for my great sadness, it was no longer a secret. After externalising it in the sessions I was able to view the problems objectively and this is the way we dealt with them, one by one.

When you are depressed you do not really see the world around you as it is in reality. Of course you see it, but, because of your illness, you might be inclined to add properties to it to make it more than it is or take something away from it to make it less (real). I was inclined to do this myself. First of all my therapist's name had associations and for a short time I almost thought of her as a guardian angel who had come to save me from myself (no doubt other clients might have thought similarly). You cannot really separate the therapist from the centre, they belong together, you never see them apart, and the centre also became a special place to me. I remember looking out of the waiting-room windown on my first visit. You can see a mural on a large brick wall at the end of the garden. It is a sort of magical scene, rolling green hills, a coastline, a fairytale castle and two small people travelling in a cart being drawn by what appeared to be two blue cats! I spent a long time looking at this scene. At the time the garden was bleak because of the time of year, the trees in the mural were bare too, and if I concentrated I could almost make the garden and the mural become one, the one running into the other. It was magical, like a doorway to another world and I dearly wanted to escape this one.

This escapism at the centre stayed with me even after we had put the (magic) garden into perspective. When I was on my own my problems were with me all of the time, day and night. I kept a notebook so that I would not forget any when I went to my session. When I went into the little room, it was as if I was leaving the world behind and didn't have to worry about it for fifty minutes. This was a great help because it made it easier to focus my mind on the difficulties I wished to discuss with Gabrielle.

Knowing that I was going to see Gabrielle each week enabled me to carry on – almost as normal as far as other people were concerned. I had a point in time to get to, I didn't worry about much ahead of that, and when a session was over it was only another week I had to get through. The sessions were a safety valve that stopped everything from piling up on me, threatening to engulf me.

After quite a few sessions I thought I was making progress, but I remember that some way into the therapy I started feeling worse instead of better. This didn't make sense to me – I was getting more depressed again and thoughts of suicide entered my mind, followed of course by the reasons why I should not. I felt so unhappy, I couldn't even motivate myself to do a picture and turned up at the session pictureless and very upset – it wasn't working. I told Gabrielle that I had not been able to draw anything because I was feeling so bad. I started crying. Not just because of the lack of a picture but out of disappointment in myself and the therapy. I felt so bad that I asked Gabrielle if it was possible for her to prescribe some medication for me, I needed something extra to help me through the week. 'Stirring up the sediment' was the metaphor Gabrielle used to explain how bringing problems to the surface so they can be dealt with would make me feel worse. She asked me to hold on for a week. What could I do? Seeing as it was only a week, I said I would try. That week was a very miserable and wretched week for me and it took a lot of getting through. I didn't think I could do it but I did. This crisis was a watershed in many respects. It was a turning point because it made me realise that my depression would not last forever, it was like riding out a storm – I had to be strong and persevere, and this is an attitude I have continued to take.

As the therapy progressed I was spending more and more time on the pictures I was taking into the session. I have to admit that in some way I was trying to impress Gabrielle, in a similar way that I had tried to impress teachers when I was at school. I was looking for some kind of gratification for my effort and hard work, recognition for being the most hard-working client that attended.

I never actually set out to do a picture of Gabrielle. The therapy room was being moved to a larger one at street level and I thought maybe I could produce another picture for the wall downstairs. Gabrielle had said to me at the last session that I had nearly reached my age, that is, my emotional age was catching up with my real age. She had been asking me to do some pictures around the theme of my therapy and I had sort of been putting it off – it was too difficult. It seemed about time that I tackled this task so I started making small sketches for a composition. It needed to show the therapy room that I had become accustomed to, it needed to include the open window with a bright clear sky outside, Gabrielle and myself had to be in there of course and perhaps the picture done by another client which had been some inspiration for me. I sketched around this and could not come up with a composition that expressed the relationship between all these things. So I just homed in on the two things I was most familiar with – Gabrielle's face and the window. Once I had finally decided to do this I became quite engrossed in the problem it posed – how to do a portrait when you have no visual material to hand, no model, no photographs or preparatory sketches.

Oddly enough, it wasn't too difficult and I was really pleased with the result. I thought I had captured her likeness pretty well. I thought it quite an achievement and I hoped Gabrielle would receive it well. I didn't think the picture would be of much use at the session beause it had turned out so different from the original composition I had envisaged. At the same time I was feeling pretty low. I was feeling depressed because, in addition to the usual mass of college work, I had also promised a friend of mine that I would design an album cover for him. Everything was starting to feel hopeless and pointless because I didn't think I could cope. I still did not have much confidence in my abilities and on that day I did not even want to go back to college. On the train on the way to the session I remember thinking how fortunate I was that I was going to see Gabrielle. At the session Gabrielle told me that I appeared to have plenty of energy. I was surprised and told her that I felt tired but Gabrielle said she meant creative energy and that gave me some confidence with which to go back and attack my work.

When I brought the drawing of Gabrielle out I could see how wrong it was; however, I still liked it as much. I thought I had captured something of her character (or what I saw of it anyway). Gabrielle said that I had been 'benign' in my drawing. I didn't think so, I thought she was pretty. She asked me why I had not put myself in the composition – had I felt overwhelmed? I didn't think so, maybe I was getting bored with always putting myself into my pictures and it was time to look at things outside myself. In that respect it was my first picture of this type.

What Gabrielle said about me feeling overwhelmed made me think. Why did I not have any fear of being involved in a relationship with her? I knew it was because I would never allow a relationship to develop in the first place. Therefore I had nothing to fear from Gabrielle and felt safe. The converse of this was that I was still very afraid of relationships. Gabrielle reminded me that I should spend some time with friends and we agreed that I had reached a point where I could 'start building again'. Although I agreed, I still felt as though I had a lot of catching up to do (ten years) and this made me feel inferior. When Gabrielle asked me how I was making progress in this area I always had the same excuse . . . 'College work'. My fear of relationships made me protect myself, I allowed my college work to take up all of any spare time I might have had. That way I never had the time to socialise, ensuring that I never got to know anybody, and nobody ever got to know me.

I felt somehow better in myself after attending the session, as I usually did, and as usual I tried to hold on to this better feeling and use it as a strength to see me through to the next session. On some occasions Gabrielle and I might have had different views about what a picture meant and how it related to my situation, but I always felt better to some extent and usually left with food for thought. Trying to remember what someone has said to you when you are depressed is not easy; nothing is as easy as it used to be. So I decided to make notes after each session. By writing down Gabrielle's comments I hoped to put them more firmly in my mind.

As time progressed, the frequency of my visits changed, initially out of necessity. I could not afford to miss a morning at college every week so I went every fortnight, which wasn't so bad as my college work kept my mind occupied nearly all my waking hours. The first time Gabrielle brought up the subject of 'finishing the sessions' I panicked. Visiting the centre on a regular basis had become an integral part of my life and I was worried about losing it. I told Gabrielle that I really wasn't ready and Gabrielle reassured me that they could continue as long as I needed them to but it was something that I should think about. The idea frightened me and I didn't really want to think about it at all. The oddest thing was that I ended up finishing the sessions myself. It had taken over two years to rebuild my confidence and self-esteem to a point where I thought I could cope in the real world and start all over again, without making the mistakes I made before, and towards the end of this time I felt the need to make pictures less. I drew for pleasure rather than to illustrate problems. Indeed, I seemed to have less problems as time went by; or was it that problems just didn't seem so terrible to me any more? So it was I who ended up telling Gabrielle that I thought I didn't need to attend any longer. I was pushing myself a little into this and wasn't totally convinced that I was making the right decision so I also asked if, should I ever need to, I could come back and see her again. I was worried in case after leaving the door was closed to you as a client. Apparently it wasn't and that made me feel more comfortable with my decision.

I had imagined I would want to take all the work in my portfolio with me when I left. I was surprised with myself that not all the work was as precious to me as I thought it would be. Gabrielle sat with me and we went through it. I had been quite prolific during my therapy and there was a mass of work. I picked out the pictures that meant the most to me or those that I considered to be 'good' in an artistic sense. The rest I left behind in case they might be of use to other clients in some way. I did not take all of the best pictures: two of the best were on the wall of the therapy room; that was where they were intended to go, and remained to say I had been there.

On that day Gabrielle showed me a picture of hers. It was in conte crayons, the medium which she had suggested I use in order to loosen up and the style reminded me of Chagall. I was quite impressed – I thought it was very artistic and realised that Gabrielle herself was a very creative person. Gabrielle told me that she would not have shown me one of her pictures before and I knew then that I was no longer a client.

THERAPIST'S RESPONSE

Kim's relationship with me was to evolve and change over time. In the early days, he was suspicious of what therapy might 'do to him' but there was also a strong part of him that felt 'time was running out' and that he needed an 'anchor'. Combined with genuine fears and anxieties about engaging in the therapy, there was a genuine desire to change his life. He was ready and receptive for the therapist to reach out to him and understand his experience.

At first he was formal and rigid in relating to me. He communicated his despair. He had become cocooned in an isolated world. In spite of this, there was a chink through which light could get. He desperately wanted someone to take an interest in him, show concern and carry some belief in what he could do. He could not believe that he was worthy of the time and would frequently check whether I considered he was wasting my time as there were others in more urgent need than himself. He was not important enough to be taken seriously, which was a profound fear for him.

My being a female therapist seems to have been less intimidating for him. I was committed to try to understand his experience through his eyes and try and enter with him into understanding his world. My thinking was informed by the work of Kohut (1972) and his use of empathy and Orbach and Eichenbaum's work on the counter-transference (1993). By trying to experience how Kim felt, I was not merging with him as one person, as he had felt in relationship to his mother. I tried to imagine how he experienced himself and then to understand this in terms of our relationship. My two guidelines were the use of empathy in attempting to enter his world and using my own feelings as an indicator of the communication from him as to what he was feeling. It was what happened between us, and between us via the image, that was the foundation of our work.

My role was not just to contain and survive his feelings. It was the living relationship that was a central part of the whole experience. Orbach and Eichenbaum (1993) write very clearly on this, saying we are not simply the sum of clients' projections, we as therapists are an important part of the relationship. They write about 'how we make us of ourselves as objects, but simultaneously return ourselves as subjects. As the subject we experience a version of that feeling state and then give it back to them in a digestible form' (Orbach and Eichenbaum 1993). This interaction has been central to our work together. We would move in and out of the process, with the third party in our relationship being the picture.

The image making seems to have reduced some of the intensity of the initial relationship, which might have been an important developmental stage for Kim. He was able to turn his back to me in the session and then talk when he felt ready. Making the image provided him with thinking time and allowed him to prepare what he was going to share with me. This enabled him to feel more in control, which initially contributed to his feeling of safety as the image became the transitional space in the dialogue we would have together.

The therapeutic task was to create an environment in which he could feel able to let down some of his defences and share some of the hidden and troubled thoughts that he had covered up over the years but which had cumulatively led to the build up of his crisis. The creation of a safe environment was to be a result of the consistent relationship I would offer him. In time I was to learn of how, in his pursuit of the perfect image, he cut himself off from all relationships, forcing himself to live in his fantasy and becoming totally alienated from the real world. Central to the relationship was that he should feel that the therapeutic space was his special time where he could explore his hidden feelings and would not be intruded upon by my emotional needs. He could determine how the time of the sessions were to be used for himself.

As Kim felt anxious and frightened about the encounter in the early days of therapy, I was very aware of how sensitive he was to my intrusion. He had felt invaded by the previous therapist and thus had reinforced his defence structure. The opportunity of making pictures allowed the transference to be communicated by the image. This was to diminish its intensity and allowed the possibility of it being understood and integrated. Tranferred directly on to me, Kim might have felt the need to defend against it. The transitional space of the making of the image allowed the possibility of recognising some of his earlier patterns of relating.

What I recognised about the relationship with Kim was that I experienced a transpersonal quality. I could understand his struggle because of my own anxieties about being engulfed and invaded by a maternal figure. I understood my own feelings of being swamped and my search for a non-merged separate sense of myself. Through my own therapy over the years, I had begun to understand the need for a boundary, a skin between myself and another significant relationship, and how, without this separate sense of self, it left me feeling vulnerable. The exploration of my own creativity had helped to develop my sense of self and maybe these aspects of my internal process communicated themselves to Kim and allowed another level of communication that is not always available in therapeutic relationships.

Kim was to move from feeling suspicious and mistrustful of me to an idealisation of the relationship. This was intensified by his extreme isolation and his desperate need for a connection that would give his life some anchorage. I was aware that it was possible that he was repeating earlier patterns in which he searched for an idol: someone whom he could imitate, taking on their persona to help him deal with the overwhelming feelings of emptiness. If the relationship was built on 'idolisation' rather than idealisation, Kim would be at risk of feeling the overwhelming sense of depletion once the relationship had ended. What I hoped for in our relationship was that Kim would find a way of taking in the relationship, so that it would exist inside him as a template for future relationships once therapy had ended. The experience for Kim would not be one of imitation but introjection. I hoped that he would be able to absorb and integrate something more real and permanent for himself. If Kim had remained stuck in an idealised transference this would have not allowed him to go through the process of separation and finding a separate sense of self. It would have left him feeling strengthened but an empty vessel when the therapy ended.

At the time I thought the process of idealisation was serving another function. It was allowing Kim to form an attachment to me. This enabled him to reawaken some 'frozen feelings'. It allowed him to experience emotions towards me which could then be transferred to relationships outside. He no longer felt he had to be cocooned, closely encased for fear of rejection and ridicule.

The idealisation was to allow the process of identification. My sense of him at this stage was that he did not have to be on his guard, suspicious in some way that I might wish to expose him. It allowed him to experience me as an ally, someone who was on his side. This early attachment enabled him to tolerate some of the images expressed in the previous sessions in his dreams. One image suggested that I had in some way exposed him, making a 'bloody and messy' scene for him. He could tolerate this as he trusted me sufficiently to know that I was not there only to rip him apart.

While Kim was beginning to make new relationships on the outside, he was still very wary about how much of himself he felt able to reveal. I still represented the place where he was able to expose parts of himself which he felt unacceptable to others. While this perhaps was an appropriate developmental phase in therapy, I hoped in time that he would feel that the world outside was a place where he was able to share an honest picture of himself. This would diminish the importance of our relationship and prepare the ground for ending.

Although Kim was taking more risks with relationships outside, he still feared intimacy. In his relationships with women he still feared the possibility of humiliation and making a fool of himself. He felt safe in the relationship with me and did not fear ridicule but it was important for him to move from idealisation to seeing me as a real person and a woman. While he invested me with the power and authority, he did not facilitate the possibility of owning this for himself.

Kim made a number of pictures that represented this struggle. This picture (Figure 12) served to focus the dilemma for him of how to see me as a person. He drew it from his imagination and at the time he could not see me, he had no picture of me, he merely had the picture in his mind. He has drawn me with a steady gaze, a generous mouth and a fine bone structure. Grey hair appears above the temple of the forehead. I am wearing large silver earrings and from the centre of the paper is a burst of silver light. The dominant colours of the picture are purples, blacks and silver grey. The picture bears quite a resemblance to myself and the earrings are a regular part of my appearance, but the image conveys a radiance, confidence and a wisdom which suggests to me that he is still caught in an idealising transference.

The picture gave us the opportunity to explore our relationship and how he perceived me. He acknowledged that he still felt that I carried the knowledge and wisdom in the relationship and he still felt he owned very little for himself. The recognition of this helped de-mystify the process as we explored the significance of our relationship. His fantasies about me, once placed on paper, were to diminish. I was to become a real person, separate from him and someone he could see and reflect upon. He was beginning to be no longer merged but separate from me.

When presented with a picture of myself, I wanted to think about my own response. I do see it as an idealised picture as there are white rays coming out of my face almost making a radiant feeling. The size of the mouth seems to suggest that it may have reflected the importance he attached to my words. The sense that he is trying to flatter or please me or portray me still in an idealised form was very much around. However, I felt that he had finally come to trust me enough to take the risk of placing the relationship on paper and that gave us the opportunity to explore this further.

The power of this image had the effect of turning any fantasies he had about me into something concrete. The making of the image was to coincide with the diminishing of the idealising transference and suggested a more interactive process. It was the beginnings of him increasingly looking to the outside world and establishing the foundations of relationships with students at college. I had the feeling that it was the catalyst for him to feel able to let go of his total dependency on me as central focus, as other areas of his life were beginning to take on greater importance.

OVERVIEW

The process of the therapy is clearly described in both accounts. It is interesting how much the experiences reflect and confirm each other – both therapist and client are very much in tune with each other. The relationship within the therapy had enormous significance for Kim. It is as if he had invested it with the same importance as a young child all pervasively involved with and attached to mother. We have seen how this has developed and can understand the significance of this in his ego development. Klein describes the introjection of a 'good' mother as a fundamental factor in development. The capacity of the ego to do this, she suggests, is innate, but

> If the mother is taken into the child's inner world as a good and dependable object, an element of strength is added to the ego. For I assume that the ego develops largely round this good object and the identification with the good characteristics of the mother becomes the basis for further helpful identifications. A strong identification with the good object makes it easier for the child to identify with a good father and later on with other friendly figures.
>
> (Klein 1959: 6)

For this attachment to the therapist to diminish, Kim needed to make other significant attachments and there were now signs that the foundations and preparations were beginning to happen. Looking at the detail of the process over time, we can see clearly how this has happened as the transference both to the therapist and within the image is worked through towards a resolution.

In the previous session described, the process of separation in the dreams has enabled the relationship with the therapist to become conscious. The dream images represented the fragmentation of different aspects of the therapist. Aspects of 'helping' and 'hurting' were significant issues in the dream material. The portrait now consolidates these into one person, the therapist, and this is where the real focus of the therapeutic relationship rests. Kim describes how he struggles to 'compose' the image of the therapy relationship and ends up with a picture which is just of Gabrielle and the window. This is important as these were the aspects of the room that Kim noticed on first entering the art therapy room. At the stage of therapy he has now reached, by putting these two together in a conscious way, he has a sense of integration but he also has the feeling of being low and depressed on its completion. The therapist has become a 'whole' object rather than a part object for Kim and as such both good and bad aspects are integrated together and he can feel both love and hate for her. The toleration of these ambivalent feelings, which Klein describes as the depressive position in the infant's relationship to mother, brings with it the feelings of loss and sadness as the infant becomes aware of the guilt about the destructive feelings previously felt towards mother. This is one way of understanding that Kim brings both happiness and sadness into the session.

This can be understood in another way. The baby is, at first, fused with the first object or mother, but then, as he comes to 'see' it, he can begin to make sense of it, understand it as a separate object and therefore separate from it. As Gabrielle points out, the image of her enabled her to become real and so the fantasy about her could thus diminish and he could begin to understand his feelings towards her. In the same way as he had made a self-portrait, so making the picture of the therapist had enabled her to become real and also someone separate from him. He was discovering that he could relate to her as a human, not a non-human or alien, as in the dream. This process of differentiation is particularly noticeable as he describes the fact that he and Gabrielle might have seen different meanings in the images and this suggests now his ability to tolerate difference. The therapist also describes how she attempts to help him differentiate or become a separate person in his own right.

The image (Figure 12, 'Gabrielle') itself suggests care, observation and a sense of radiation. Kim describes the difficulties he had in visualising her and also in his struggle to portray the therapy experience. He could visualise the therapist; painting a picture of her fixed this in his mind and she remains open and available to this communication. The centre is equally important as a safe place in his mind. The imminent move of the art therapy room causes some anxiety and there is a feeling he wants to preserve this space in the picture. He does this by linking the therapist and the window together in his finished image. The face of the therapist is not as carefully executed as the self-portrait. The blurredness might imply less clarity of feeling and perhaps a residual sense of fantasy or anxiety as his feelings shift away from himself towards another love object. Kim describes how he feels that this picture is different in this respect, and it is the first time he has done one of this type. Kim's description of his experience highlights the process of idealisation: the therapist for a time was his 'guardian angel', which led to dependency and a sense of deepening despair. In the one session he brought no picture, the emptiness prompted such anxiety that he perceived Gabrielle in a different role in his request for medication. The art therapist moves to 'doctor' in his confusion but Gabrielle responds and holds this anxiety and does not react to it by doing something for him. By staying with his difficulties, she did not fill the space or plug up his problem, and she did not collude with his anxiety to be given something. She offered reliable, predictable space that was a containing experience for him to feel safe. This was sufficient to hold him until the following week. As he describes, this was ultimately a strengthening experience. He was able to work through his difficultes for himself and survive.

Throughout his description, we come to understand how crucial was this therapeutic space for Kim. It is made possible through his experience of consistency over time in the therapeutic relationship. The knowledge that he had a regular contained space was for Kim a new experience and an important one for an internal growth. As Kim implicity trusts Gabrielle, he can risk relying on the therapy and he knows that she is able to tolerate the most unacceptable aspects of himself. The boundaries have been tested and he feels totally contained. He can then introject the worst aspects of himself and so can tolerate them for himself. The portrait demonstrates that he has internalised her in this way, the image of the therapist is inside him. He points out how he begins to hold on to her thoughts through notes, which is another indication of this process.

Anyone looking at this picture might respond to it as the portrayal of Gabrielle as an all-devouring, overpowering, consuming woman and in a sense the image also conveys these ambivalent feelings for Kim. The image cannot swamp him and he can therefore express any fears of being swamped which are safely contained in the image. He is pleased with his picture, writes about thoughts of seeking her approval and makes a comment about his emotional age. Perhaps this is his sense that he is not allowed to have 'adult' feelings and is in touch with the realisation that he is 'growing up' as he relates to the therapist almost like a teacher, or as a man towards a woman. As the sexualised nature of the transference becomes acknowledged, he is able to make these connections with his own sexual feelings towards the therapist. We can see in the dialogue that this was raised in the session and worked with, as their relationship becomes the focus of the material. Kim describes Gabrielle as 'pretty' but as his ideas of having a more intimate relationship with her surface, he dismisses this as an impossibility. His fantasies about the therapist have become reality as the transference is worked through. The issues have been met fact to face as his feelings towards the therapist are fully explored. With the realisation that no sexual relationship will happen with the therapist, it is now possible for him to think about Gabrielle's comments about other relationships. Deep down he struggles with conflicting feelings which are becoming clear in his need for relationships which coincides with his deep fear of them.

Gabrielle's response to the image is once again to remain open to Kim's understanding of the content. She describes her own thoughts in understanding Kim's process and her identification with him in terms of her own sense of being invaded but also in her understanding that it is also possible to be a separate person for him. Here we can see the importance of the therapist having undergone her own personal therapy to be able to understand these experiences for herself. The danger otherwise is to project all these aspects into the client and not acknowledge where they belong. Counter-transference responses are useful indicators for understanding the client's experience and, unless the therapist is clear in her own mind, the experience of them can be blocked off and denied within the therapist and therefore within the therapeutic space as they are struggling to surface.

This is particularly important with a portrait of a therapist. These images are bald statements and usually convey the direct struggle for the client in clarifying feelings towards the therapist and the emotional relationship between them. Anyone not skilled in understanding this process might react superficially with thoughts about personal likeness, accuracy of features and so on. These are attempts to hide some embarrassment about feeling exposed or being confronted by the reality of how one looks. For the therapist to come so 'alive' in the work can cause discomfort and anxiety and therapists working with video will understand how it feels to be so openly portrayed for all to see. There is a sense of 'exposure' which is something on which Gabrielle comments.

Interpretation of surface detail is therefore not helpful but what is important is to get the sense of what the image depicts and what the client is trying to communicate. Gabrielle fully understands the essence of these reactions and how to respond appropriately. She is able to feel that Kim is grappling with his relationship with her. How does he feel really about her and what can he do with these internal feelings that are generated within the transference love?

At first, Gabrielle was idealised by Kim and she describes how she feels this has been worked through. As the idealisation shifted in the therapeutic relationship, he was able to take aspects of the encounter inside himself and therefore idealisation in other relationships outside was also to shift. His feelings towards the therapist can be contained and processed within this intense encounter and these again can be taken into relationships in the outside world. He could learn from this experience, and once again we understand how useful are Bion's concepts of alpha and beta functioning. Instead of projecting his thoughts and feelings onto the therapist and other relationships, he could begin to establish real contact with human experience which does involve complex, sometimes ambivalent and conflicting emotions. This acknowledgement of the therapist was very important at this stage for Kim. The split-off parts of himself could be integrated and strengthen him in relating to others. The therapist became a whole, real person in his mind and, as he was able to experience the full force of his feelings for the therapist, he could begin to engage and establish relationships in this way in his own right. Just as meaning becomes established by identifying an experience with words, Gabrielle could be identified and clarified in Kim's mind as a separate entity, not merged with him, but as a person and a woman in her own right. At the beginning of their relationship, they were not so much in tune with each other but fused together in the process. Now, there is a sense that therapist and client are more in harmony but separate. By having this experience of separateness, he could then feel he could function separately and without her and thereby feel it is possible to leave.

We also notice, in this quite painful process of ending, how the therapist was able to see the end before Kim but the thought was held by the therapist until he was ready to take it in for himself. He could thus be facilitated to manage his own ending of therapy which helped him with feelings of loss, rejection and emptiness which he was in touch with when he first brought the portrait to Gabrielle. The process also changed the use of the image for Kim. The end of therapy meant that he could draw in a different way for a different purpose and, in the same way as with the therapist, resolution has taken place in his feelings towards the pictures he had made in therapy. He was able to leave some of them behind, as he was able to leave the therapist, but he would also take some with him as he would take away aspects of the internalised therapist. Resolution of the transference to both image and therapist has taken place. This is most significantly pointed out by Kim in his experience of the transition from being a client to being a person and artist in his own right as Gabrielle also feels able to share her images with him. The role of therapist–client shifts significantly to that of two artists discussing their work. This is the confirmation that Kim neded for himself, although he describes how scary he finds it; it is also important that there is a possibility of seeing Gabrielle again if he should feel the need to.

Figure 13 Leaving the maze.

Chapter 12

Leaving the maze

Kim came to art therapy sessions weekly for eighteen months. When he was feeling strengthened, no longer overwhelmed by his depression, less isolated and setting the foundations for real relationships, it was agreed by both Kim and Gabrielle that he would come on a less regular basis. He was now entering his second year at college. For the next six months he attended on a fortnightly basis which was then renegotiated to a monthly session. This continued until the end of that year when he left college and therapy was terminated.

Over this time, Kim wrote many letters which proved to be an extended component of the therapy and the following extracts document this period of work.

KIM'S VOICE

After substantially reducing the sessions I found a lack in my life . . . a lack of someone to talk to about the various situations (they were problems to me!) that cropped up as I was endeavouring to make my way on my own. I still did not have the courage to talk to my old friends about things like this. I never had in the past, and most of them did not know that I had been attending therapy. I was keen to keep this quiet if I possibly could. I didn't want too many people to know about my dark past. I just wanted to pick up my life where it left off as if nothing had happened. What I was missing was the opportunity to bring my anxieties out into the open and externalise them as I had being doing at the sessions and which had been constructive in dealing with them. When I felt this vacuum particularly acutely I wrote to Gabrielle. They were sort of rhetorical letters for which I did not necessarily require or expect a reply – appreciating how busy Gabrielle is – but just writing them, knowing they would be read and understood was a help. Often the crisis which prompted me to write passed within a few days and made me feel a little foolish. I did not want Gabrielle to think that I was 'crying wolf', but I still wrote to her afterwards to let her know that things were better in case she was wondering how I was coping.

At this time I was also using the act of letter writing as a way of occupying myself – time that I knew I should have used to go out and get the hang of mixing with people again. The time that had been filled with college work was now filled with letter writing – not just with job letters (even though these often took a couple of days each week). I was also keeping in touch with three people who had been at college with me, a new friend who lived in the north of London and a penfriend in America. I managed to fill most of my weeks with letter writing while I was waiting for that job opportunity to present itself, and with full-time work came the curtailing of my correspondence to most of these. It was not that I no longer had any problems, it was more that I had less time to worry about them and they seemed less important than putting everything I had into the start of my new career. I suppose my fear of not being accepted in the graphic design industry was greater than my fear of not being accepted in a relationship in terms of failure and the purpose of my life. With this accomplished, my confidence was greatly increased. I did not necessarily want to 'be my job', and I knew that it was important that I did not let my identity rely on this totally. However, it was a starting point that has enabled me to begin integrating with the world in a way that I never have before and I took the responsibility of meeting and talking to people upon myself.

Sometimes I still find the world a difficult place to live in. I can't honestly say that I do understand what motivates the majority of people on this planet but I do find life more bearable now.

THERAPIST'S RESPONSE

Changing the sessions to a fortnightly basis was a joint decision made for a number of reasons. Kim was less isolated and had established a number of social relationships. He was still struggling with intimacy but he had spent time thinking about this with me in our discussions through the images. Kim was keen to reduce his time coming to the clinic. On one level, he said he was finding difficulty taking time out of college, but perhaps of greater significance was his desire to see if he could cope without coming so regularly. He felt ready to rely on his own resources and he was laying the foundations for a life outside. We made an agreement that he could write or telephone for an appointment should he feel the need and in this sense I felt I was still providing a firm safety net into which he could fall if necessary. It was as if Kim had reached the adolescent stage in his relationship with me.

The letters Kim wrote reflect some of his struggles and his attempt to make sense of the complexities of intimate relationships, not to hide behind a manufactured mask but to take the risk of revealing the real Kim. The disappointment, the frustration, the hope, the affection, the confusion were all part of the process. Therapy cannot change the on-going passage of experiences but, as a result of the process, hopefully the client feels more able to survive difficulties, feels strengthened and not overwhelmed by hurdles. In Kim's case he was more able to analyse his experience so that he did not always turn difficulties in relationships against himself. He struggled to make sense of the part he played and not always to internalise the blame by attacking himself.

The first excerpt is the final paragraph of a letter in which he describes his struggle with a friendship with a girl which he would like to make more intimate. He feared messing it up. Kim's previous pattern had been to withdraw from anything he did not understand and, although this was gradually changing, he still feared rejection. It was painful to clarify the truth about her feelings but it was often easier to live with the reality of what was possible as opposed to being trapped in a fantasy. He had learnt from a friend that she did not want to be his girlfriend and this is how he conveys his disappointment.

> I may phone you at Lancaster Rd on Thursday just in case you are there because I don't know how I'm going to cope with this one. I had spent so much time and energy to try and build up a relationship that wasn't just based on fantasy and it's still going to come to nothing. What am I doing wrong? I am a very sad young man at the moment.
> Thank you for reading this.
> Best wishes,
>
> Kim.

The next letter refers to the hurt that Kim feels as a result of the rejection. He recognises that previously his 'false self' had not allowed him to feel the pain of rejection. He writes about the defence of the image and not himself. While in the past this had worked as an effective defence mechanism, protecting him from the pain, it had also prevented him 'feeling'. He had been 'numbed' and cocooned from his emotions. Kim recognises this in the letter and, although this is a letter to the therapist, he is also writing to himself. He acknowledges that he has not been able to talk to anybody else about his anxieties and he is still looking for a person with whom he can share his vulnerabilities. In this sense, he is using the therapist as a transitional space with the world outside.

> In retrospect I can see how even if I was disappointed with a girl's reaction (or lack of it) to the 'image' I put up I never felt it directly. The affection or rejection was always projected onto the image, or at least I felt it was (even though that may not have been the case) and so it only touched me indirectly and nothing was ever intense. True I never felt any true affection and that didn't really bother me because all I was concerned about was the way that (or who) I looked like, but

at the same time I never experienced a rejection of myself, only the image I put forward.

Don't worry, I don't think I'm likely to slip back into my old ways even though the thought has crossed my mind. What would it achieve? NOTHING. I apologise for the 'bad news' but it had to be done. I feel a bit guilty about this and maybe it's because of the time of year. It seems important that my feelings and thoughts about this relationship and the trouble it causes me be put 'on the record'.

Once again my pride has stopped me from talking to anyone about this this evening. I have a suspicion I would be liable to get very upset if I did but conversely I may be bottling it up which may (or may not) do me no good.

Also I find it is screwing up my working attitude again and is making me feel less professional after the boost to my ego at the interview. Why does life have to be so complicated?

I hope I will have a better grip on things by the next time I see you. I need to have because there is a lot of work for me to get through before returning to college.

I apologise again for writing, perhaps we could discuss this guilt feeling I have the next time we meet. Maybe I need to hold on to the 'doctor–patient' relationship a bit longer.

Best wishes,

Kim.

Later the same month:

> Yes I am upset, but more angry, not with myself though, which I would have been in the past.

In this excerpt, he is struggling with not turning his frustration into an attack on himself. The previous pattern of blaming himself, internalising it and later becoming depressed is changing in that this is a reality response. Placing it outside himself might allow him to make sense of the experience in a different way.

Eight months later.

> I am feeling fairly good about myself at the moment (despite not securing a job yet) in my appearance and my ability to cope in social situations. I am, however, still having trouble with young ladies though. I had to curtail my last meeting with Deirdre as she was just being too tactile and intense and was making me very nervous indeed.

In the following session, Kim talked about his anxiety about having a sexual relationship and his fear of being overwhelmed and invaded. His response was to withdraw. He feared messing it up and being rejected and this was explored in his discussions with me. I was holding in mind the notion of readiness. On the one hand, he needs to take a risk in the hope of a good enough experience but if he does not feel 'ready' or sufficiently good about himself, it might go wrong and he will feel more vulnerable about himself. We worked on the notion that it is quite appropriate to feel nervous at the moment and if it does not go as he would hope then it is all material for learning.

The following month:

> Even though I cannot tackle another large oil-painting at the moment I have started working on a composition (though I don't want to get it totally out of my system before I've started painting it!) and have enclosed a copy of the rough sketch . . . which of course may differ greatly from the finished piece. I should like my next painting to include the expression I have learnt to release over the last couple (three?) years and try, this time, to leave some blank canvas . . . just to break my obsession with covering every square millimetre and help make my own conceptions about art more flexible. The idea in the sketch is mainly to do with my obsession about time, how it both holds me back as well as being my main motivator – the exaggerated mechanisms of the watch is behind me pushing, but my arms are bound into the straps which are holding me back. Other elements I would like to incorporate are my past history and future hopes, we shall see.
>
> Once again, many thanks.

Kim enclosed a rough sketch with this letter. In his recognition that he has to cover every inch of paper, he is referring to his need to have everything planned, in control. In the past, he thought it gave him greater security but, in practice, it led him to great disappointment and frustration when things did not turn out as expected. His planning of his world had not allowed things to happen. While Kim now recognises this part of himself, the paradox is that the planning of the image to allow something to happen is perhaps a contradiction of what he is trying to achieve.

In the excerpt from the next letter, Kim directly expresses his need to see me but he sends the letter second class. Although he is clearly in some distress, he had learnt to contain his anxiety and not feel overwhelmed by it.

> Dear Gabrielle,
> I was going to write to you for an appointment because I had been feeling very unhappy (to say the least) lately. Close to tears in fact. As it happens I'm not feeling too down at the moment but I thought it might be prudent for me to see you because, despite the fact that I believed I was coping very well with my unsatisfactory situation, the couple of tearful moments I have had may be a warning that I am kidding myself!

The letter ended as a catalyst to explore together the notion of 'kidding' himself. It was not a new theme in our discussions, but it highlighted for Kim that it was possible to feel a different range of emotions, which may feel as though they contradict each other. The fact that Kim had felt tearful on occasions did not nullify the fact that he had been coping. Kim's expressions of vulnerability did not wipe out his expressions of strength. Kim was more accessible to these ideas and, although it was a struggle to integrate them, it gave him the possibility of not having to punish himelf so acutely when his life was rough.

> I have met a very intriguing young lady at church. We have been out together for a meal and a drink and . . . well it's difficult for me to say what's happening as I am a bit confused (again) myself and I don't want to make a fool of myself so soon again. I will be making another date with her though because I do enjoy her company or rather I find her company very calming/relaxing. Unusual for me eh! Oh, by the way, I am being myself as well – odd really.
> Best wishes
>
> Kim.

OVERVIEW

The letters speak for themselves and so detailed comment is hardly necessary. This use of letter writing to manage the ending of a therapeutic relationship is clearly outlined and Kim tells us how helpful he finds it. He could still hold the therapist in mind, he had internalised her, and could therefore take more risks in the world outside. He could have a discourse in his head or on paper with the therapist. It was the beginnings of the process of separation and the redirection of his emotional investments.

There is a sense that he is working through some of his fantasies about being intimate with the therapist which again was an important aspect of their communication. Even though he has stopped seeing her regularly, this seems to help him think about the real possibility of developing intimate relationships outside. As Gabrielle remarks, it seems as though their relationship has reached an adolescent stage and real ambivalence about leaving. Maintaining some contact puts off the time for actual separation but also allows Kim the time to prepare for this fully. His final comments suggest that this has been clearly achieved, but he is able to acknowledge this with the full awareness of the reality of this situation.

Chapter 13

Conclusion

The overall process of therapy and its termination can be understood in a theoretical context but, equally, this is no substitute for the reality of the ending of the therapeutic relationship. There are therefore two 'endings' given here – the first will be in the form of the dialogue recorded two years after treatment ended. The other is the theoretical understanding of this process.

The first-hand account that the dialogue offers us indicates that this is not an ending but actually a beginning. The reality of Kim's recovery towards growth and a more solid sense of self has been described in his images, letters and in the dialogue. These are 'three voices' in themselves and are testament to his experience. We thus have a full account of how Kim sees the future as well as his experiences of art therapy in hindsight.

DIALOGUE BETWEEN KIM, GABRIELLE AND TESSA TWO YEARS AFTER THE END OF THERAPY

Tessa: I am interested to explore a bit further the relationship between you and Gabrielle. What was it that allowed you to sufficiently trust her that it would in time allow you to change? Was there something particular in the relationship?

Kim: My previous therapist had been a man. I did not want to be like a man. Men for me were scruffy, messy and treated women badly. I had a problem with having a man as a therapist. I didn't really trust him. One day he asked me directly whether I was homosexual. He just came straight out with it. I had read Freud and did not like him having him quoted at me like that. I could not be pigeon-holed. I started to play a game with him. I was not going to engage in the therapy so I decided to select my answers. He was not going to catch me out. I ended up being referred here.

Tessa: Was it because Gabrielle was a woman that made the real difference?

Kim: Yes, it was. I didn't have an ego problem with Gabrielle. I did not feel I could say to a man I was feeling bad and I wanted to cry. With a woman my pride was not at stake. I was not being judged by another man. I was not in competition with Gabrielle. I could say what I needed to say without feeling I would be judged or laughed at.

Tessa: Do you think it was because Gabrielle was a woman or was there somethig particular to the relationship.?

Kim: Perhaps what seemed to make a difference was that Gabrielle seemed to understand that I was in a terrible situation. She seemed to communicate that she wanted to help me. I felt her sincerity. I always attended the sessions with the idea in my head that she wanted to help me.

Tessa: Would it have been easier to be angry with a male therapist?

Kim: It is not really in my nature to be angry, that is not how I express myself.

Gabrielle: Were there things you were sitting on when you saw me?

Kim: No, on an occasion when a particular picture meant something to you and not to me, I would say, I don't remember ever really leaving the sessions feeling frustrated, even when I was very depressed. I remember coming to the session asking if you could contact my GP for medication. I remembered you telling me that it was because very painful material was beginning to surface and that I was going to feel worse and that it was all part of changing. You suggested that I tried not to take anything for the next week. This allowed me to leave feeling it was possible.

Gabrielle: That was later on, wasn't it? In the early days it was more difficult for you.

Kim: As you say, it takes a while to get the hang of things. Later on I could make more use of the sessions. Being very depressed made it very difficult to disagree. Making the pictures was enough at the time.

Gabrielle: That sounds right. It took time before you felt able to challenge me. As you became clearer about who you were and what you thought, it became easier to stand out and say what you wanted. It was part of becoming stronger. I saw that as a very important part of the therapy, getting more definition of yourself.

Kim: Yes, I agree with that.

Gabrielle: Tessa and myself have discussed together a great deal where the transference might lie in the pictures and in the relationship. By this I mean the ideas that all of us have very important relationships with significant figures in authority. The most significant are usually with our parents. It is not unusual in our adult relationships to recreate these relationships. By this I mean we unconsciously treat these adults as if they were an early parental relationship. If this was true it would be possible that you would sometimes relate to me 'as if' I was your mother. What do you think about this idea? Do you think this was going on in the relationship between ourselves.

Kim; No I don't think I ever saw you like that. Besides I would never talk to my mother. I was able to tell you things, confide in you, in a way I would never have been able to do with my mother. I saw you more like a 'confidante'. When I was younger I had had quite a lot of female friends. So it was not difficult to talk to a woman.

Tessa: Another thing Gabrielle and I have talked about in our practice is the idea of making the picture at home and what that might have meant to you.

Kim: I wanted to spend more time on the pictures. The session is only an hour and I wanted more time to talk. If I did the picture at home it meant I had more time to talk it through with Gabrielle. I felt the need to do so and so it felt more productive to me. Yes, I was nervous at first, making a picture in front of Gabrielle, but most of all it was the pressure of making a picture in twenty mintues and then having less time to talk. One of the things I really felt I gained from therapy was the ability to visualise. What I see in my mind I can put on to paper.

I think that depressed people are introspective. I don't think it is a bad thing to have something to think about and do at home.

Gabrielle: That could be quite an albatross. It can feel like a pressure to have to produce something to bring for the session. Did you ever feel like that?

Kim: There was one occasion when I didn't bring a picture. It was never a burden for me. I made the picture because it was what I wanted to do, and was important for me.

Gabrielle: Yes, one of the things I thought it did best was that it allowed you to hold onto the session; because you were working at home, it made a connection for you between what happened here and how you were managing outside.

Kim: Right. I suppose in some respects I was taking the session home with me. I put a lot of thought into the pictures. I would still be thinking about the session while doing the picture. As for my talent, I didn't think my pictures were very good when I first came. They were very childish. I was attending evening classes to try and improve my drawing.

Gabrielle: Certainly one of the things that changed very radically was that your pictures became more alive. They had a flatness, a deadness to them when you first came.

Kim: There was a lack of confidence. I saw my pictures as 'bad' because I was depressed.

Tessa: Did your parents or family encourage you to draw as a child?

Kim: Yes, I always had pencils, felt pens and paints available. I was given the materials and the encouragement. When I was back at home and coming to art therapy I would wait until everybody was in bed and I would start making my pictures at about 11 o'clock.

Gabrielle: Was there something inhibiting about drawing in front of others?

Kim: Then I think there was. Now I am quite happy to draw in front of others. There was a lack of confidence.

Gabrielle: It is reminding me of when you first came. You were going to evening classes and people would come up to you and say your work was good and you thought they were humiliating you.

Kim: I didn't think they were being sincere.

Gabrielle: Perhaps what was different then was that you thought people were getting at you.

Kim: Yes, it was difficult to accept what people were saying.

Gabrielle: Can I ask you what it has been like being involved in the book and how you have found the change in the relationship.

Kim: I didn't find it very difficult because I felt we had come to the end of the client–therapist relationship.

Gabrielle: Yes it is quite different – it is a different relationship as a therapist. You didn't know if I had a partner, if I had children, you knew very little about me. I was a much more neutral person. In this relationship you have been able to see different bits of me. I wonder what that was like for you.

Kim: It is interesting. I can see that you really are 'human'. Before, you were always 'doing your job'. I thought you did your job well and that gave me confidence to attend. Now I see you have quite a good sense of humour. I don't know if you had to suppress that during the work, because you are quite a funny lady. You have also shown me some of your pictures. I didn't know you drew then. You introduced me to conte crayons. I see you use them also.

Gabrielle: It is interesting what you say about humour. I'd like to think that I didn't hide that part of me. Perhaps when the person who is seeing you is in a high anxiety state they could easily misinterpret humour and feel quite persecuted.

Kim: Yes, I think that is true. I think if you had been laughing I might have thought it was at me.

Tessa: We have a different role sitting here together compared to just being in the role as therapists. Would it be useful now to look at the pictures. Perhaps we could talk about certain ones.

Kim: (holding the maze picture (Figure 13 'Leaving the maze') This was one of the most contrived pictures. I was feeling much better at the time of this one. It started off as a self-portrait, but it went wrong. I then decided to do a maze over it, for no particular reason. There is always the allusion to the maze of the mind. There is the shadow of myself locked into the maze and a small shadow of myself leaving the maze. Often in my pictures I try to visualise something. In this particular picture, if you consider the shadow to be the dark depressive part of my nature, then I was leaving it behind. I would like to have thought that was the case. It was locked away and never going to trouble me again. Of course I know that depression isn't like that. The picture of course is contrived but it is a visualisation. It didn't come from the heart. I don't know whether it should go in [the book] as a result.

Tessa: What I found interesting is that there is a connection between the beginning and the end. You started off with something you thought was not very genuine, then you moved towards some very deep work such as the dreams which seemed to be coming right from the inside. Then you emerge out into a more reality-based situation with you and Gabrielle. The end has to be a superficial image because you have to surface, a bit like coming out of the swimming pool. I would be in favour of it going in, just letting it stand as a visual image of this process.

Gabrielle: We did think about this at the time, this notion of you hoping to find that the dark side would be bolted away for ever. This was one of the issues we tried to think about, how you hoped it would not reappear. The difference, however, might be that these shadows might reappear. What you do know now is that within yourself there is the possibility of not being so overwhelmed. It could not be left in the cupboard, bolted away for ever, but it might frighten you less. It would, however, always be visible.

Kim: Yes I remember discussing this. Although I was adamant I had overpowered it. I had won the battle.

Gabrielle: You consider the image not to be authentic because it is derivative. Well I think that lots of our images are derivative of what we see around us. What was important was what you made of it and what meaning it had for you.

Kim: But compared to all the other things that came completely out of my head, it was not as genuine.

Tessa: What I find interesting is the connection to the outside world. That you can walk out and you are making a connection to the outside of the therapy.

Gabrielle: I think we were just beginning to talk about ending at this point. It was when you produced this image that we were able to begin to really think about it.

Kim: Yes, that seems about right at the time.

Gabrielle: You were trying to tell me about your 'readiness' to work towards ending.

Kim: I don't think I was aware of it consciously at the time.

Tessa: It would be interesting to think about the ending. You had been seeing each other for about eighteen months. Can you remember what it felt like?

Kim: Well, despite what I said about this picture, my fear of ending the sessions was: what would I do if I didn't attend? I had all kinds of visions of getting into trouble. Gabrielle said I could make contact whenever I wanted but I was reluctant to give up coming to the sessions.

Gabrielle: Well, it was the issue of readiness. We began to think about reducing the intensity of the relationship and you were beginning to look at the world outside. I think, however, over the next year we retained quite substantial contact. The other area we developed our communication was through writing letters.

Kim; Yes, that's right. I stopped attending on a regular basis but I'd keep Gabrielle informed both when good and bad things happened. Letting you know seemed important even if I didn't need help. I still wanted you to know.

Tessa: I'd like to know what it is like to think about these pictures now.

Kim: The art therapy sessions helped me enormously with my depression which was terrible. You can also see how my drawing skills improved, so when I look at these pictures now I have a sense of satisfaction.

Tessa: My response to some of these images is that they are quite gruesome. Do you have a feeling response to them now?

Kim: The feeling response I had to them at the time was sort of exorcised through them if you like. I am reluctant to let them go because they are important to me. I want some to be on the walls in the clinic because other people's pictures had an impact on me and I want to leave something behind for other people. I don't like to pore over them and get moody. I want to keep them all together. It is a history. I feel a sense of achievement and satisfaction when I look at them – they mark a crisis in my life when I thought I couldn't carry on, there was no pleasure in anything, nothing to look forward to, no point to my life. And here I am now at the start of a new career where I feel I have something to offer and with many possibilities, which, even though I am not a pop star, is still exciting. I don't have intense feelings about them anymore, but, if it embodies something and speaks to other people, then I'm very happy.

Tessa: They convey what happened to you without words.

Gabrielle: As you were talking I'm remembering how, when you first came, you felt you were empty and had nothing inside. Today I hear you saying you have 'Too much to say'. The area which we used to spend a lot of time thinking about was your fear of relationships, making contact, being intimate, I suppose I would like to know what you feel about that now.

Kim: I have been accused of being too serious. One of the reasons I got depressed was that there did not seem to be any point in my life so that was a disappointment and affected my confidence. Now I know I have more to offer through therapy and college. I've replaced my desire to be a pop star with being creative. I've had to accept that I need to be able to have relationships. Now I even engage the local shop-keepers in, dare I say it . . . chit chat!

Gabrielle: I was meaning more than that. What about in friendships, having girlfriends? Is that something you now find satisfying or would you still rather not take the risk of having relationships?

Kim: Yes, I think I am still trying to get the hang of it. I'm not sure I handle relationships as I should. I have a lack of experience. I do have conflicts. But I never really wanted to be alone – on my own all the time. I was just frightened before. When I was depressed I was caught up with the ideas of the suffering artist; the sage and the hermit who live in solitude. Because of that, they had an air of mystery about them. I used my depression as an identity. I was gathering that cloak around me, it was something familiar. If that was taken from me I had nothing left. There was a fear of being well again. Maybe in some perverse way I wanted people to feel sorry for me. I suppose it is the opposite side of charisma. Being depressed was something about me that people would notice. Obviously I was not going to get a partner interested while I was so self-absorbed. While I was on my own I never went out looking for a relationship.

Gabrielle: I remember we would have a lot of discussions about your fear of messing it up and your feeling that you had nothing to offer.

If people get too close to you, you feared they would see through you and you would be transparent.

Kim: Yes, I remember. I'm glad you reminded me of that. When I was obsessed with image I wanted lots of adoring fans. When I became depressed I did not have that image any more and thought I could not possibly be attractive. The idea of a girl finding me attractive did not seem possible. Before I was depressed I was quite funny. Over time this got eroded. I think that funny part of me has come back. I still find it odd that I have a girlfriend because I'm nothing special. I suppose you have to learn to like yourself, and perhaps that is something I learnt to do in therapy. I feel more confident and at ease with myself now. I am still inclined to model my appearance on famous people who have that charisma or style which I would like to have (or think I have) myself. The difference is that now I know how this can become an obsession I make sure I keep it under control. I think this is OK as long as it is kept in check. Funnily enough, when I was back on the road to reality I did mention to my best friend John about how much trouble I had been in over the previous couple of years and he told me that he was upset because I hadn't spoken to him about my problems when I was contemplating suicide. I tried to explain how I had spent so long being somebody else that I had forgotten how to be myself. He said he didn't see the conflict that I had, to him I was someone who is naturally inclined to imitate other people. It is the way I am.

Tessa: My final question is I was wondering what it was like when you finished therapy. How you felt afterwards.

Kim: I thought I would not look back when I finished therapy. Perhaps like the picture in the maze. It was not like that. I often felt like I would like to come back. I had to push myself, it has been difficult. I no longer feel I need that help. It was a very gradual change, a very gradual building of my confidence. The change has been great, but it has taken a long time.

For the record I feel it is important for me to say something about the way my feelings towards my parents have changed. With hindsight I can see that my perception of their lack of interest in my mental state was probably caused by the fact that, because of the barriers I erected around myself, nobody could perceive that there was anything wrong – I didn't give any signs or ask for help. I may have felt bitter at the time, looking for someone to blame and sometimes thought that, as parents, they should have seen the dead end route that I was heading down and advised me. They were probably just giving

> me the freedom that they thought I wanted, being generous as they always were. Since ending my obsession with image I feel more down to earth and am happily rebuilding the relationship with my parents and trying to make it more how it should have been. I feel a lot closer to them, and the rest of my family, these days.

THREE VOICES

We have had the privilege of following one man's intense, internal journey on his path towards creative living and health. Looking at the process so closely in this way gives a unique insight into hopelessness and helplessness and how gradually, over time, hope and a future can become a reality. The images Kim produced during the period of his therapy provided him with a voice and thus the communication of his experience became a possibility for him.

As well as giving an account of his intense therapeutic experience, the images told his life story. The pictures illustrated this and the therapist responded to them as they spoke rather than knowing about the events beforehand. Kim was thus able to tell her his story.

The images tell us about how he arrived at this point and the series of works he created are important to consider, as they so graphically portray the past experiences in his life and also the sequence of events within the therapy. The movement from the 'diagrammatical' to the 'embodied' image demonstrated the way that Kim made the important step of emotionally investing in his images and allowing his feelings to surface in this way. The transference was communicated through the image as well as in the relationship with the therapist and Kim was then able to make sense of the powerful and confused feelings with which he was struggling.

Let us look at the overall process. Initially, the 'early image' portrayed an outer image, or what we have come to understand as a 'false self'. 'Trap' conveyed the beginning of coming to terms with his experience of his family and the next images describe how mother became the focus for his difficulties. After he worked through feelings towards mother, the 'Harlequin', or cocoon, shifted the focus onto the person of the therapist as the transference process became more clarified. 'Breaking out' of the cocoon enabled Kim to examine his relationship with women, as the transference shifted to a more sexualised base. As he no longer feels the need to rely on the individual therapist/mother, joining groups, in 'Against the tide', became the next issue of concern and whether they can be experienced as sustaining or swamping. Connected with this, the dream images 'Under the skin' and 'Barrier' enable deep feelings to become conscious and these are a real expression of his anxieties and fears. This marks the beginnings of separation from the therapist. 'Gabrielle' becomes the focus in the next image as he can begin to clarify his feelings about her. Image and therapist are joined in this process, as the transference, no longer kept separate between image and therapist, comes together and is resolved. He can now begin to think about 'Leaving the maze'.

The notion of working through, as described at the beginning, has been demonstrated. We can see how central is the function of the image within the relationship in terms of holding and working through of the transference particularly in relation to mother. As Kim describes, he did not experience Gabrielle directly 'as if' she was his mother. The transference to mother was contained in the image. The therapist was perceived more as someone he trusted while his feelings about mother were expressed through the images and could thus be worked through in this way. Subsequently, fear of annihilation, having nothing inside and other deep anxieties connected to his fragile sense of self, his relationships and inner feelings of conflict, anger and guilt come to be expressed. The images literally become three-dimensional as an internal space for thinking develops. He can hold feelings inside and make sense of them rather than projecting them out onto the therapist. It is here that we see how the alpha functioning becomes a reality, by holding on to feelings and allowing them to be stored, and he can now learn from experience. Previously his reaction to feelings with beta elements projected them out on to the therapist and others, most importantly on to his idols. We can understand how this must have left him feeling so empty inside.

From the central voice of the image, the therapist also has a voice in terms of her experience of the therapy. Again we hear from the dialogue how she saw and felt what happened.

> In the long term I carried the belief that it was the beginnings of him 'unpeeling' his false persona and the early days of being able to establish a more authentic foundation. It was for Kim very frightening. He felt empty inside. His feelings of worthlessness were associated with knowing that, once his shell was taken away, he would have to learn how to fill himself up with something real, that had real meaning for him. Kim at this time did not know that this was possible and that he had any potential for this. He had however communicated to me a genuine creativity. I knew from working with other clients and from my own experience that such self-expression can offer, in time, a richness that leaves one no longer depleted. Kim made his pictures alone. His isolation distorted his internal and external world as he had little means of testing reality and this had led to a deeply sensitised persecutory internal world. I sensed the making of images marked the beginnings of sharing all these internal thoughts and fears. Much of this internal world had become unavailable in language but could be symbolised and therefore expressed in images. The act of making the image was, for him, an intense solitary experience and allowed him to prepare deeply

> for the sessions. It would allow some of his internal preoccupations to surface but, if left alone with them, although now externalised on paper, there was still the possibility of their remaining distorted. By bringing them to the sessions, he was able to share with me, to allow the persecutory thoughts, the false mirroring and the distortions to be explored. It was this two-stage process of making the image in his own isolation and then sharing it with me that was allowing the internal perception of himself to change.
>
> I felt that what was beginning to happen, slowly, was that in the making of the images he was finding a way of expressing himself that was involving the placing of himself – often his real self – on paper. There was an authenticity and genuineness emerging in the pictures he was doing and this was gradually beginning to permeate through to this other work that he was preparing for his portfolio at college. Kim was to recognise that one of the side effects of being in art therapy was that he was to find a way of putting himself into the pictures: a form of self-expression, creative literacy that was to influence his work profoundly.

By holding the hope, and recognising his creativity, Gabrielle used her counter-transference response which enabled the confirmation of Kim's needs and established a sense of self. Making the images, and their acceptance within the sessions, also had the effect of working through some 'exhibitionistic tendencies', allowing a greater cohesion of the self. It seems this concept of the 'good enough mother' or experience of mother as an infant is a central theme in this clinical material and its understanding by the therapist enabled Kim to make sense of it himself.

Taking the voice of the overview, there are many aspects of theoretical understanding that can be brought to this material. We can see how the application of Winnicott's ideas of false and true self has been central to the understanding of the change over time. Kim was able to find a fragile but real self under the masks he had been presenting to the outside world for years. Kim describes how he comes to recognise this for himself and see that his masks have served as a real detachment from the relationships he now seeks. One is reminded of how the death masks of Tutankhamun were so influential in his thinking as a growing child; it seems that this had a significant impact on him.

Another way of looking at Kim's progress in therapy can be understood in terms of the Kleinian view of ego development in the movement from the paranoid–schizoid position, in which feelings are split between good and bad objects, towards the depressive position in which feelings of ambiguity, loss and guilt can be tolerated. Winnicott (1954) sees the depressive position in emotional development as an achievement and this is also how Kim's progress can be understood. Just as the Oedipus complex characterises normal or healthy development of children, 'the depressive position is a normal stage in the development of healthy infants (and so also is absolute dependence, or primary narcissism a normal stage of the healthy infant at or near the start)' Winnicott (1954: 262). Winnicott points out that 'we know that in many adults who are in therapy, the approach and reapproach to the depressive position is an important feature of the therapy which is an indication of progress and at the same time implying earlier failure at this developmental stage'. Kim was able to reach this stage, or the 'stage of concern' as Winnicott prefers to call it, by being able to tolerate ambivalence, difficulty and conflict without reverting back to an old pattern of dealing with it which was to internalise the guilt and become depressed. Klein also makes a similar point.

> In normal development with growing integration of the ego, splitting processes diminish and the increased capacity to understand external reality, and to some extent to bring together the infant's contradictory impulses, leads also to a greater synthesis of the good and bad aspects of the object. This means that people can be loved in spite of their faults and that the world is not seen only in terms of black and white.
>
> (Klein 1959: 9)

This feels useful in summing up the experience of Kim at the termination of his therapy. Another central feature in the process was the expression of the Oedipal conflict. It seems that the relationship between Kim, Gabrielle and the image has provided the structure of the Oedipal triangle and enabled some degree of resolution to take place. Being unable to separate from mother, merged and overwhelmed at father's absence and passivity, meant Kim did not, at the normal developmental stage, experience the frustrations and rage about his parents' partnership and his exclusion. His developmental task was to achieve this separateness. Through his images and relationship with Gabrielle he was able to achieve a separate sense of self. As a result, Kim was to learn to relate to his parents as separate people and not as an extension of himself.

Gabrielle often questioned in her mind why there was not more emphasis placed on Kim's relationship with father. Within the process it is noticeable how Gabrielle indirectly took on the role of father in the transference while mother depicted in the images was held more centrally in mind in their discussions. In her thinking Gabrielle felt that the material Kim brought seemed to suggest a constant preoccupation with mother and may give an indication that Kim was unable to see a role for his father in the family. The absence of an authoritative voice was clearly a major factor in his development. Kim's own experience of father was of a passive, non-involved man who tended to remain distant. However, in the background he seemed in some way to hold the family together, even as the absent 'bread winner' or 'provider' for the family.

While the images did not express aspects of Kim's relationship with father as directly as that with mother, the live relationship with Gabrielle came to represent the father. It was as if Gabrielle became the alternative father who also provided the structure – she set firm limits and boundaries for the sessions, created a secure and safe environment in which to work, which provided the outer frame for the therapy to proceed. The deep exploration of the relationship with mother could follow as a result. As the therapy developed, and this was worked through, father came more clearly into focus, particularly in the dream material with the emergence of some angry feelings. As Kim explains, it is not in his nature to be angry but he could begin to express these feelings through the images and they became acknowledged in the work. He was therefore not overwhelmed with his anger but could externalise it, without losing control. Gabrielle remained able to tolerate angry, gruesome and painful material as Kim grappled with this. Indeed there were thoughts in her mind about surgeons and this actually emerged into the sessions in Kim's request for medication as Gabrielle became the 'doctor' in his desperation. Gabrielle 'took' the control over this issue, and by holding the boundaries and therefore his anxiety, did not collude with his need for action. She was also able to support his need to find accommodation, holding him in his search, until he felt more settled and able to explore his dreams.

All these aspects of the relationship reflect the holding of the paternal function and were most helpful for Kim. This seemed important, particularly in connection with the previous therapist who was male. Kim had experienced him as intrusive and perhaps too penetrating in his questioning. Certainly the experience of being 'pigeon-holed' was one aspect that Kim found most unacceptable at this early stage, as he so acutely feared humiliation which was a direct transference to father. Having finished working with this therapist, maybe somewhere in Kim's mind he had 'killed him off', and so a degree of Oedipal resolution had already taken place on seeing Gabrielle. This certainly seemed to be connected to Gabrielle's experience, in that she felt it was relevant that she was a woman, and these points are interesting to think about in hindsight.

It might be that some aspects of the process of this clinical material have not been sufficiently emphasised or picked up on, but in the beginning we invited the reader for their thoughts and likewise we now do the same. Some interesting points spring to mind, such as how difficult Kim found the experience of the male therapist. General considerations of gender difference might have been explored in more depth given the problem of the Oedipal conflict. This connects with Kim's angry feelings towards the therapist and how the emergence of aspects of negative transference was not directly addressed. Some pointers to this could be seen in Gabrielle's approach which might not have allowed sufficient empathetic failure, but this is unlikely because in most therapeutic encounters there is frustration and disappointment. Kim's explanation for this is that he does not remember leaving the sessions more frustrated than helped, although there were times he wished he had said something different at the time. This would seem to be because his transference to the institution and the therapist very quickly became centred on his expectation that the sessions would be helpful.

Another thing that is powerfully at work in any creative process is the experience of rage, anger, frustration in the actual act of making the image. Kim's feelings may have been expressed and worked through in the making of the picture. He clearly describes this process, particularly as the therapy develops and he invests his emotions in his images. As we see, many of Kim's angry, more persecuted feelings came to the surface particularly towards the end in the dream images, the content of which could be seen as savage and vicious. He was in touch with this and he describes how he can disassociate from these very strong negative feelings which give him pain; this is also an aspect of the real experience of his illness and how he 'learnt' to cope with the pain by disassociation. This is an important insight in itself and linking this in his mind enables him to take on the negative feelings himself towards the end of the therapy. The resolution of the transference thus takes place, the idealisation diminishes as he is able to feel anger, guilt and contradictory feelings as Gabrielle becomes a person and a woman in his mind. It is interesting to think about how different approaches affect this outcome.

Another interesting issue that needs thinking about, and is central to our understanding of this case, is the fact that most of the images were made outside the session time. We can see from his account how this resonates with Kim's experience of his art lessons at school. While we know the reasons for this, it is worth considering whether, in response to the feelings of invasion, this could be understood as an empathetic response in Gabrielle's understanding of his fear of being overwhelmed or collusion to avoid difficult and negative feelings emerging in the session. The effect on the process was a kind of regression to an important point in Kim's life. We note that it was after Kim left school and abandoned the idea of developing art as a career that the masks became intensified, triggering his depression. We might consider what would have happened if this approach had not been adopted. One answer is certainly that we would not have the privilege of being able to work with such well-executed images, which is of central importance to Kim and how we have come to know him.

What is important is that it seemed to be the right therapeutic approach for Kim, and Gabrielle's sensitivity to this enabled him to work through his difficulties without feeling too persecuted and overwhelmed by the experience. He could remain sufficiently in control for him to be able to do this himself. We must remain open to different ways of working without too rigidly sticking to technique, and, by thinking about these, they can continue to inform our understanding of the process and outcome of therapy. Listening and learning from the client after all is crucial in the development of our practice.

In Kim's case the articulation through his images facilitated the necessary communication for his voice to be heard. Hearing his voice through her own understanding of the creative process in therapy, Gabrielle provided a safe space in which his images and words could be contained and understood and in this way his experience was confirmed. She also carried into the relationship the hope and the belief that he could change. Within the relationship, this consolidated his own understanding of his experience and feelings grew from this in the establishment of his sense of self, the recognition of his real self, from which point he could begin his life in the real world. Therapy is 'not simply the sum of our clients' projections, but we are an important part of the relationship' (Orbach and Eichenbaum 1993). The three voices were the pictures, the client and the therapist and the triangular relationship between them.

‘Sometimes I still find the world a difficult place to live in. I can’t honestly say that I do understand what motivates the majority of people on this planet but I do find life more bearable now.’

Kim Terry, 1992

References

1 INTRODUCTION

Meares, R. and Hobson, R.F. (1977) 'The persecutory therapist', *British Journal of Medical Psychology* 50: 349–59.

Orbach, S. (1989) 'Emptiness Within: The Search for Intimacy', paper delivered in Auckland, New Zealand.

2 CONTEXT OF PRACTICE: SOME THEORETICAL CONSIDERATIONS

Bion, W. (1961) 'A theory of thinking', in E. Bott-Spillius (ed.) *Melanie Klein Today*, London: Routledge.

Bion, W. (1962) *Learning from Experience*, London: Heinemann.

Bion, W. (1977) *Seven Servants*, New York: Jason Aronson.

Case, C. and Dalley, T. (1990) *Working with Children in Art Therapy*, London: Tavistock.

Case, C. and Dalley, T. (1992) *The Handbook of Art Therapy*, London: Routledge.

Dalley, T. (1984) *Art as Therapy*, London: Tavistock.

Dalley, T. *et al.* (1987) *Images of Art Therapy*, London: Tavistock.

Klein, M. (1957) *Envy and Gratitude*, London: Tavistock.

Kohut, H. (1971) *The Analysis of the Self*, New York: International Universities Press.

Kuhns, R. (1983) *Psychoanalytic Theory of Art*. Colombia: Colombia University Press.

Milner, M. (1955) 'The role of illusion in symbol formation', in E. Bott-Spillius (ed.) *Melanie Klein Today*, London: Routledge.

Mitchell, S. (1988) *Relational Concepts in Psychoanalysis (An Integration)*, Cambridge: Mass.: Harvard University Press.

Sandler, J., Dare, C. and Holder A. (1973) *The Patient and the Analyst: The Basis of the Psychoanalytic Process*, London: Maresfield Reprints.

Schaverien, J. (1992) *The Revealing Image: Analytical Art Psychotherapy*, London: Routledge.

Segal, H. (1957) 'Notes on symbol formation', *International Journal of Psycho-Analysis* 38: 381–7.

Segal, H. (1975) 'Art and the inner world', *Times Literary Supplement*, 3827 (18 July): 800–01.

Simon, R. (1992) *The Symbolism of Style*, London: Routledge.

Winnicott, D. (1960) 'Ego distortions in terms of true and false self', in *The Maturational Processes and the Facilitating Environment*, London: The Hogarth Press and the Institute of Psycho-Analysis, 1965.

Winnicott, D. (1963) 'Communicating and not communicating, leading to a study of certain opposities', in *The Maturational Processes and the Facilitating Environment*, London: The Hogarth Press, 1965.
Winnicott, D. (1981) *Playing and Reality* London: Penguin.

4 EARLY IMAGE

Sandler, I., Dare, C. and Holder, A. (1973) *The Patient and the Analyst: The Basis of the Psychoanalytic Process*. London: Maresfield Reprints.
Schaverien, J. (1989) 'The picture within the frame', in A. Gilroy and T. Dalley (eds) *Pictures at an Exhibition*, London: Tavistock.
Schaverien, J. (1992) *The Revealing Image: Analytical Art Psychotherapy*, London: Routledge.
Winnicott, D.W. (1960) 'Ego distortion in terms of true and false self', in *The Maturational Processes and the Facilitating Environment*, London: The Hogarth Press and the Institute of Psycho-Analysis, 1965.

5 FAMILY PICTURES

Bion, W. (1962) *Learning from Experience*, London: Tavistock.
Casement, P. (1987) *On Learning from the Patient*, London: Tavistock.
Klein, M. (1959) 'Our adult world and its roots in infancy', *Human Relations* 12; in *Our Adult World and Other Essays*, London: Heinemann, 1963.
Kohut, H. (1984) *How does Analysis Cure?*, University of Chicago Press.
Kohut, H. and Wolf, E. (1978) 'The disorders of the self and their treatment: an outline', *International Journal of Psycho-Analysis* 59: 413–25.
Rifkind, G. (in press) 'Containing the container. The work of staff consultancy groups: exploring the relationship between group analysis, self psychology and the consultation process', unpublished thesis.
Schaverien, J. (1992) *The Revealing Image: Analytical Art Psychotherapy*, London: Routledge.
Winnicott, D.W. (1965) *The Maturational Processes and the Facilitating Environment*, London: The Hogarth Press and the Institute of Psycho-Analysis.
Wolf, E. (1988) *Treating the Self: Elements of Clinical Psychology*, New York: Guilford Press.

6 RELATIONSHIP WITH MOTHER

Bion, W. (1967) *Second Thoughts*, London: Maresfield Reprints.
Klein, M. (1959) 'Our adult world and its roots in infancy', *Human Relations* 12; in *Our Adult World and Other Essays*, London: Heinemann, 1963.
Kris, E. (1975) *Psychoanalytic Explorations in Art*, New York: Schocken Books.

7 IN THE COCOON

Bick, E. (1968) 'The experience of the skin in early object relations', in *Collected Papers of Martha Harris and Esther Bick* Strath Tay: Clunie Press, 1987.
Bion, W. (1977) *Seven Servants*, New York: Jason Aronson.
Cornwell, J. (1984) *The Survival Function of Primitive Omnipotence*, London: Tavistock Institute.
Freud, S. (1914) *On Narcissism: An Introduction, Standard Edition* 14: 75–6.
Klein, M. (1975) *Envy and Gratitude and Other Works 1946–1963*. London: Hogarth Press and the Institute of Psycho-Analysis.

Kohut, H. (1972) *The Analysis of the Self*, New York: International Universities Press.
Schaverien, J. (1992) *The Revealing Image: Analytical Art Psychotherapy*, London: Routledge.
Winnicott, D.W. (1958) 'The capacity to be alone', in *The Maturational Processes and the Facilitating Environment*, London: Hogarth Press and the Institute of Psycho-Analysis, 1965, pp. 29–36.
Winnicott, D.W. (1981) *Playing and Reality*, Harmondsworth: Penguin.

8 BREAKING OUT

Fairbairn, W.R.D. (1952) *Psycho-Analytic Studies of the Personality*, London: Tavistock.
Levenson, E. (1991) *A Perspective on Responsibility: The Purloined Self.* New York: Contemporary Psychoanalysis Books.
Milner, M. (1987) *The Suppresed Madness of Sane Men*, London: Tavistock.
Orbach, S. and Eichenbaum, L. (1993) 'Feminine subjectivity, counter transference and the mother daughter relationship', in J. Van Mensverhulst (ed.) *Daughtering and Mothering: Female Subjectivity Reanalysed*, London: Routledge.
Segal, H. (1957) 'Notes on symbol formation', *International Journal of Psycho-Analysis* 38: 391–7.
Segal, H. (1975) 'Art and the inner world', *Times Literary Supplement* 3827 (18 July): 800–1.
Storr, A. (1972) *The Dynamics of Creation*, Harmondsworth: Penguin.
Winnicott, D.W. (1963) 'On communication', in *The Maturational Processes and the Facilitating Environment*, London: Hogarth Press and the Institute of Psycho-Analysis, 1965.

9 SEARCH FOR IDENTITY

Winnicott, D. (1951) 'Transitional objects and transitional phenomena', in *Through Paediatrics to Psychoanalysis*, London: The Hogarth Press and the Institute of Psycho-Analysis, 1982.
Klein, M. (1959) 'Our adult world and its roots in infancy', *Human Relations* 12; in *Our Adult World and Other Essays*, London: Heinemann, 1963.

10 DREAMS

Bion, W.R. (1977) *Seven Servants*, New York: Jason Aronson.
Case, C. and Dalley, T. (1992) *The Handbook of Art Therapy*, London: Routledge.
Casement, P. (1987) *On Learning from the Patient*, London: Tavistock.
Ehrenzweig, A. (1967) *The Hidden Order of Art*, London: Paladin.
Freud, S. (1912) 'Recommendations to physicians practicing psycho-analysis', *Standard Edition* 12: 109–20.
Hobson, R. (1974) 'Loneliness', *Journal of Analytical Psychology* 19: 71–89.
Kohut, H. and Wolff, E. (1978) 'The disorders of the self and their treatment: an outline', *International Journal of Psycho-Analysis* 59: 413–25.
Meares, R. and Hobson, R. (1977) 'The persecutory therapist', *British Journal of Medical Psychology* 50: 349–59.
Schaverien, J. (1992) *The Revealing Image: Analytical Art Psychotherapy*, London: Routledge.
Tracey, N. (1991) 'The psychic space in trauma', *Journal of Child Psychotherapy* 17(2): 29–42.

Winnicott, D.W. (1965) *The Maturational Processes and the Facilitating Environment*, London: The Hogarth Press and the Institute of Psycho-Analysis.

11 RELATIONSHIP WITH THE THERAPIST

Klein, M. (1959) 'Our adult world and its roots in infancy', *Human Relations* 12; in *Our Adult World and Other Essays*, London: Heinemann, 1963.
Kohut, H. (1972) *The Analysis of the Self*, New York: International Universities Press.
Orbach, S. and Eichenbaum, L. (1993) 'Feminine subjectivity, counter-transference and the mother–daughter relationship', in J. Van Mensverhulst (ed.) *Daughtering and Mothering: Female Subjectivity Reanalysed*, London: Routledge.

13 CONCLUSION

Klein, M. (1959) 'Our adult world and its roots in infancy', *Human Relations* 12; in *Our Adult World and Other Essays*, London: Heinemann, 1963.
Orbach, S. and Eichenbaum, L. (1993) 'Feminine subjectivity, countertransference and the mother–daughter relationship', in J. Van Mensverhulst (ed.) *Daughtering and Mothering: Female Subjectivity Reanalysed*, London: Routledge.
Winnicott, D.W. (1954) 'The depressive position in normal emotional development', *British Journal of Medical Psychology* 28.

Name index

Subject index